To: _____

From: _____

Date: _____

100 VOICES

100 VOICES

Words that Shaped Our Souls
Wisdom to Guide Our Future

COMPILED BY

ANNE CHRISTIAN BUCHANAN

AND

ÐEBRA K. KLINGSPORN

FRONTPORCH

BOOKS

100 VOICES

WORDS THAT SHAPED OUR SOULS, WISDOM TO GUIDE OUR FUTURE

Compiled by Debra K. Klingsporn & Anne Christian Buchanan
Art & Design by David Carlson Design
Photos by Archive Photos

Copyright © 1999 by FrontPorch Books, a division of Garborg's
Published by Garborg's, Inc.
P.O. Box 20132, Bloomington, MN 55420

ISBN 1-58375-478-4

CONTENTS

Introduction

100 Voices began as a simple idea: a decade-by-decade compilation of voices worth remembering. The project seemed like a simple idea—100 years, 100 voices—until we began our immersion into a century's worth of published works by writers, theologians, historical figures, teachers, pastors, and poets. The idea no longer seemed so simple. How to narrow the possibilities? How to decide who made the cut? How to determine the focus, the criteria? And once the voices were selected, how to choose which words from the many they wrote or spoke?

As we began this project early in the last year of a century soon gone, I, Debra, stood in the hallway of my home late one evening looking into the bedrooms of my sleeping daughters, feeling overwhelmed by the prospect of what I'd agreed to do. Every night for more than a decade I've stood for a few moments in the same place, watching two little girls sleep, thanking God for the gift of another day, another day to be their mom. That night as I watched them sleep, I realized they will cross the threshold of womanhood as one century gives way to another.

The twentieth century has been the historical backdrop for the lives of their great-grandmothers, their grandmothers, and their mother. A century that began with the telegraph as the most technologically advanced means of communication is ending with the reality of a new technological frontier–the global explosion of the Internet. Clarity came as I stood in that hallway praying, as I have nearly every night of their lives, *Oh God, let them grow in your grace.* I knew this work was ultimately for them. If I could give them only a handful of wisdom, what words would I choose for them to take into adulthood? More than gifting them with great literature, poetry, wit, or wisdom, I would want to provide them with some spiritual direction. I would want them to know that a life lived with God at the center is a life lived fully, passionately, joyfully. They will hear many voices growing up, many claiming "spiritual truth." If I could hand-pick a few from this century, a few who spoke with timeless wisdom, who would they be?

100 Voices is compiled with that question as the undergirding framework for this book. We have not tried to point the way to God; rather we have tried to select words that invite one to discover the spiritual side of life. As we've read through works from the past ten decades, we asked, How have those who've shaped our souls tried to put words to the divine-human encounter, how do we deepen the experience of prayer, how— in the midst of conflicting, competing, distracting realities—do we turn our hearts toward God?

Our hope is that the voices you encounter in these pages

will introduce (or reintroduce) you to spiritual mentors who have left their mark in profound ways, spiritual guides who have much to offer any generation. Yet we recognize that these selections are only gleanings, glimpses into the wealth of wisdom that lies at the heart of the twentieth century. We have not tried to be exhaustive or complete. Although our daughters may have provided the clarifying focus for this compilation, we have tried to select excerpts and quotations that appeal to all ages—from those who were young with this century to those who will grow old with the next.

Recognizing that a limited compilation such as this is inherently subjective, we would like to identify a few factors that went into the research and selection for *100 Voices.*

First, we are both Christians and that fact has informed our selections. We are also women and Americans; these realities, too, have directed our choices.

Second, with a century's worth of words from which to choose, we have decided to restrict the selections to works of non-fiction. However, we have made exceptions in nearly every decade.

Third, quotations and excerpts selected from the first seventy years of the century are not typically gender inclusive. To alter them, we felt, would not represent the century with integrity. So we have chosen to quote the words as they originally appeared.

Fourth, we intentionally looked for a diversity of voices to include, only to find that it is in the most recent decades that voices of minorities and people of color have become more widely published and their contribution recognized. Because of the brevity of this compilation and our choice to focus on widely heard voices, their representation in this volume remains relatively small.

Finally, as a general rule, we've gone by copyright dates in placing the material within a given decade. However, some quotations are placed within the decade for which that work was most representative, regardless of the copyright date.

As writers and editors ourselves, we consider this project a sacred trust, and complete our work on this volume with the prayer that these voices will continue to speak "to those who have ears to hear" for many decades yet to come.

—DEBRA K. KLINGSPORN &
ANNE CHRISTIAN BUCHANAN

Acknowledgments

We would like to express appreciation to Dr. Martin E. Marty, the Fairfax M. Cone Distinguished Professor of the History of Modern Christianity at the University of Chicago. Dr. Marty is widely recognized as a preeminent historian of religion and the role it has played in shaping the social and political life of America. During an interview, Dr. Marty walked us through the decades, offering an invaluable overview of the historical events and the religious influences that define the twentieth century. Unless otherwise cited, Dr. Marty's observations are taken from this interview.

We'd also like to acknowledge invaluable help from several people who provided significant research assistance: Dr. David Fisher, Rev. Paul Ulrickson, Rev. Richard Davis, and Dr. C. W. Christian, for resource material on Karl Barth, Henri Nouwen, C. S. Lewis, and Paul Tillich, respectively; Rev. Karen Fisher Younger for research assistance; Jessica Aubrey for research assistance in the sermons and speeches of Dr. Martin Luther King Jr.; and Jean Jacobs for biographical assistance. Finally, we have to acknowledge the help and support of our husbands, Dr. Gary Klingsporn and Dr. Stan Buchanan, for without their extensive libraries, late night queries, theological insights, and historical perspectives, this book would have been much longer in development.

Overview:

The Nineteen Hundreds

1900–1909   An Optimistic Beginning

THE CLOCK STRIKES MIDNIGHT. With the turn of a calendar page, a new century begins. From the pioneering spirit of Robert Peary, the first man to stand at the North Pole, to the Wright brothers' success with the first "flying machine"—this was the decade, the century, when anything was possible. The new century began with optimism, confidence, peace, and prosperity.

The 1900s was the decade of beginnings. Although less than 150 miles of American roads were paved, the automobile arrived and caught the imagination of the country. The cost of sugar was 4 cents a pound, butter was 24 cents a pound, and a dozen eggs cost 14 cents. The majority of households didn't have bathtubs (1 in 7 homes) or telephones (1 in 13), but that didn't hinder the spread of electricity that began to flow into homes during this decade. Evolving inventions included the telephone, typewriter, and sewing machine. Sears and Roebuck, catering to a mostly rural country, continued building a direct mail empire that would last through the entire century. Indeed, there was no limit to what humanity could accomplish—or so it seemed.

But where light shines brightest, shadows are inevitable. America had its dark side: child labor, scandals, corruption. A woman might have nine children with the hope that two would survive. The major causes of death were diphtheria, typhoid, and malaria. Pneumonia was often fatal. Yet the political, social, and moral problems were not enough to shake American's faith in the inevitability of progress. The new century gave birth to Pentecostalism, the Salvation Army, and what came to be called the "social gospel"—programs of social reform by those who believed they could bring the Kingdom of God to the social and economic order.

■　■　■

The Decade at a Glance

- 1900　Sigmund Freud publishes *The Interpretation of Dreams* in Germany.
- 1900　L. Frank Baum writes *The Wonderful Wizard of Oz*.
- 1900　Eastman Kodak starts selling a $1 Brownie camera.
- 1901　The first electric typewriter goes on sale.
- 1901　Marconi sends a radio signal across the Atlantic.
- 1901　President William McKinley is assassinated; Theodore Roosevelt becomes president.
- 1901　In England, Queen Victoria dies, ending the longest running British monarchy in history.

- 1903 Wilbur and Orville Wright make flight a reality at Kitty Hawk.
- 1903 *The Great Train Robbery* launches the film industry.
- 1904 Construction begins on the Panama Canal.
- 1904 New York City opens the first portion of its subway system.
- 1904 A woman is arrested in New York for smoking in public.
- 1905 The Yellow Pages are born.
- 1905 Albert Einstein develops his theory of relativity.
- 1906 Sears and Roebuck opens the largest business building in the world.
- 1906 Upton Sinclair writes *The Jungle,* exposing the meat packing industry.
- 1906 An earthquake hits San Francisco, killing more than 2,500.
- 1907 Picasso shocks the world with the painting *Les Demoiselles d'Avignon.*
- 1907 The Boy Scouts are founded.
- 1908 Henry Ford starts selling the Model T for $850 each—available only in black.
- 1908 William Howard Taft is elected president.
- 1909 National Association for the Advancement of Colored People (NAACP) is organized to fight social injustice toward blacks.
- 1909 An expedition led by Robert Edwin Peary reaches the North Pole.

Enduring Moments

The twentieth century looms before us big with the fate of many nations.

THEODORE ROOSEVELT
April 10, 1899

———————

No race can prosper till it learns that there is as much dignity in tilling the field as in writing a poem.

BOOKER T. WASHINGTON
Up from Slavery: An Autobiography, 1901

———————

Speak softly and carry a big stick; you will go far.

THEODORE ROOSEVELT
September 2, 1901

———————

We do comparatively very little business in cities, and we assume the cities are not at all our field.... I think it is our duty to prove they are not.

RICHARD W. SEARS
Correspondence, 1906

———————

The problem of the twentieth century is the problem of the color line.

W. E. B. Du Bois
The Souls of Black Folk, 1903

Success. Four flights Thursday morning. All against twenty-one-mile wind. Started from level with engine power alone.... Inform press.

Wilbur and Orville Wright
Telegram to the Reverend Milton Wright, December 17, 1903

Sensible and responsible women do not want to vote. The relative positions to be assumed by man and woman in the working out of our civilization were assigned long ago by a higher intelligence than ours.

Grover Cleveland
Ladies Home Journal, 1905

Come along with me Lucille in my merry Oldsmobile.

Gus Edwards
"In My Merry Oldsmobile," ca. 1900

■ ■ ■

THE NINETEEN HUNDREDS

(1900–1909)

VOICES OF THE DECADE:
An Optimistic Beginning

To be glad of life because it gives you the chance to love and to work and to play and to look up at the stars—to be satisfied with your possessions but not contented with yourself until you have made the best of them—to despise nothing in the world except falsehood and meanness, and to fear nothing except cowardice—to be governed by your admirations rather than by your disgusts; to covet nothing that is your neighbor's except his kindness of heart and gentleness of manners—to think seldom of your enemies, often of your friends, and every day of Christ; and to spend as much time as you can, with body and with spirit, in God's out-of-doors—these are little guide-posts on the foot-path to peace.

HENRY VAN DYKE
My Heart Sings, ca. 1900

■ ■ ■

It is well to remind ourselves, from time to time, that "Ethics" is but another word for "righteousness," that for which many men and women of every generation have hungered and thirsted, and without which life becomes meaningless.

JANE ADDAMS
Democracy and Social Ethics, 1902

■ ■ ■

Who seeks for heaven alone to save his soul,
May keep the path, but will not reach the goal;
While he who walks in love may wander far,
Yet God will bring him where the blessed are.

HENRY VAN DYKE
The Story of the Other Wise Man, ca 1900

■ ■ ■

FROM THE WRITINGS OF BOOKER T. WASHINGTON

My whole life has largely been one of surprises. I believe that any man's life will be filled with constant, unexpected encouragements of this kind if he makes up his mind to do his level best each day of his life—that is, tries to make each day reach as nearly as possible the high-water mark of pure, unselfish, useful living. I pity the man, black or white, who has never experienced the joy and satisfaction that come to one by reason of an effort to assist in making someone else more useful and more happy. It seems to me that one of the most vital questions that touch our American life is how to bring the strong, wealthy, and learned into helpful touch with the poorest, most ignorant, and humblest, and at the same time make one appreciate the vitalizing, strengthening influence of the other. How shall we make the mansions on yon Beacon Street feel and see the need of the spirits in the lowliest cabin in Alabama cottonfields or Louisiana sugar-bottoms?

*Up from Slavery: An Autobiography,*1901

It makes a great difference in the life of a race, as it does in the life of an individual, whether the world expects much or little of that individual or of that race.

BOOKER T. WASHINGTON
The Intellectuals and the Boston Mob, 1911

■ ■ ■

FROM THE WRITINGS OF G. K. CHESTERTON

Let your religion be less of a theory and more of a love affair.

Take away the supernatural, and what remains is the unnatural.

Heretics, 1905

Existence has a value wholly inexpressible, [and] we are most truly compelled to that sentiment not by any argument or triumphant justification of the cosmos, but by a few of these momentary and immortal sights and sounds, a gesture, an old song, a portrait, a piano, an old door.

Robert Browning, 1903

"The Christian ideal," it is said, "has not been tried and found wanting; it has been found difficult and left untried."

A thing worth doing is worth doing badly.

What's Wrong with the World, 1910

Love means to love that which is unlovable, or it is no virtue at all; forgiving means to pardon that which is unpardonable, or it is no virtue at all.

G. K. CHESTERTON
"Conversations," 1906

From the writings of W. E. B. Du Bois

One ever feels his twoness—an American, a Negro; two souls, two thoughts, two unreconciled strivings; two warring ideals in one dark body, whose dogged strength alone keeps it from being torn asunder.

The Souls of Black Folk, 1903

What did it mean to be a slave? It is hard to imagine it today.... But there was in 1863 a real meaning to slavery.... It was in part psychological, the enforced personal feeling of inferiority, the calling of another Master; the standing with hat in hand. It was the helplessness. It was the defenselessness of family life. It was the submergence below the arbitrary will of any sort of individual. It was without doubt worse in these vital respects than that which exists today in Europe or America.

W. E. B. Du Bois
Black Reconstruction in America, ca 1935

■ ■ ■

FROM THE WRITINGS OF ALBERT SCHWEITZER

I have given up the ambition to become a great scholar, I want to be more—simply a human.... We are not true humans, but beings who live by a civilization inherited from the past, that keeps us hostage, that confines us. No freedom of movement. Nothing. Everything in us is killed by our calculations for our future, by our social position and cast. You see, I am not happy—yet I am happy. I suffer, but that is part of life. I live, I don't care about my existence, and that is the beginning of wisdom.... I believe that I possess this value: to serve Jesus. I am less at peace than if my goal would be to attain a professorship and a good life, but I live. And that gives me the tremendous feeling of happiness, as if one would see a ray of light in a deep pit, as if one would hear music. One feels uprooted, because one asks, what lies ahead, what decisions should I make—but more alive, happier than those anchored in life. To drift with released anchor.

The Private Letters between Albert Schweitzer and Helene Bresslau, 1905

Those who thank God much are the truly wealthy. So our inner happiness depends not on what we experience but on the degree of our gratitude to God, whatever the experience. Your life is something opaque, not transparent, as long as you look at it in an ordinary human way. But if you hold it up against the light of God's goodness, it shines and turns transparent, radiant, and bright. And then you ask yourself in amazement: Is this really my own life I see before me?

He comes to us as One unknown, without a name, as of old, by the lakeside, He came to those men who knew Him not. He speaks to us the same word: "Follow thou me!" and sets us to the tasks which He has to fulfill for our time. He commands. And to those who obey Him, whether they be wise or simple, He will reveal Himself in the toils, the conflicts, the sufferings which they shall pass through in His fellowship, and, as an ineffable mystery, they shall learn in their own experience Who He is.

ALBERT SCHWEITZER
The Quest of the Historical Jesus, ca. 1906

OVERVIEW:

THE TEENS

1910–1919   End of Innocence

The decade began with optimism high and continuing economic growth. The country was fox-trotting, discovering jazz music, and learning to drive the more than 10 million automobiles that were now competing with mules and horses for room on America's unpaved roads. War was a thing of the past. Americans were on the high road.

"Most Americans knew that forces of evil were bad, that sin was social as well as personal," historian Martin Marty says, "but they didn't really believe the forces of evil would hold us back."

The established rules were soon to be challenged. Between women's suffrage, racial tension, and labor unrest, the American way of life was about to change. In 1910, hundreds of women marched down Fifth Avenue in New York City, demanding the right to vote, a right denied to "criminals, lunatics, idiots—and women." In 1915, widespread growth of Ku Klux Klan chapters throughout the nation led to the terrorizing of immigrants, Jews, Catholics, and especially blacks. In the first six months of

1916, our country saw 2,093 labor strikes and lockouts. Life in the United States bristled with tension.

The outbreak of World War I quickly submerged the undercurrents of change. On June 6, 1917, in the twelve hours between 7:00 A.M. and 7:00 P.M., 10 million young men registered for the draft.

The war was a noble cause for Americans; for Europeans, however, it was shattering. The Battle of Marne claimed half a million lives in a week; a million in two weeks. "Europeans had a sense of the futility of it all," Marty says. "For Americans, it didn't happen that way. We were over there making the world safe. [Woodrow] Wilson even called our boys 'Christ's soldiers.'"

Innocence came to an end in the years between 1914–1919, a time which brought the realization that "hard work, self-reliance, and faith in God is not enough."

■   ■   ■

The Decade at a Glance

- 1911   A Chinese revolution ends the 2,000-year-old Manchu dynasty.
- 1912   The maiden voyage of the *Titanic* ends in tragedy.
- 1912   War breaks out in the Balkans, setting the stage for World War I.
- 1912   Woodrow Wilson defeats Teddy Roosevelt and William Howard Taft to become president.

- 1913   The International Exhibition of Modern Art in New York City unveils Marcel Duchamp's *Nude Descending a Staircase, No. 2,* as well as other modern art, to America.
- 1913   Federal income tax is introduced in the U.S. through the Sixteenth Amendment.
- 1914   The first transcontinental telephone call is made.
- 1914   Albert Schweitzer opens a hospital in the French Congo.
- 1914   The term *movies* is coined as the motion picture business emerges.
- 1915   The *Lusitania,* a British passenger liner, is sunk by a German submarine, killing 1,198 passengers, including 128 Americans.
- 1916   Wilson is re-elected.
- 1917   The United States declares war against Germany.
- 1918   World War I ends, leaving 8.5 million dead, 21 million wounded.
- 1919   In some areas, people start dialing phone numbers without the aid of an operator.
- 1919   A world-wide flu epidemic creates an international public health crisis.
- 1919   The League of Nations is formed, but the United States refuses to join.

■   ■   ■

Enduring Moments

Business underlies everything in our national life, including our spiritual life. Witness the fact that in the Lord's Prayer, the first petition is for daily bread. No one can worship God or love his neighbor on an empty stomach.

WOODROW WILSON
Speech, New York City, May 23, 1912

In stature, grace, and hue,
In shadowy silent distance grew the Iceberg too.

THOMAS HARDY
The Convergence of the Twain, Lines on the Loss of the Titanic, 1912

I am the people—the mob—the crowd—the mass. Do you know that all the great work of the world is done through me?

CARL SANDBURG
I Am the People, the Mob, 1916

Armed neutrality is ineffectual enough at best.... The world must be made safe for democracy.

Woodrow Wilson
April 2, 1917

Let me then say, as plainly and as strongly as I can, speaking as a minister of Christ, speaking as a messenger of God...speaking in the sanctuary of Christ, that it is the high and sacred duty of the American people [to crush Germany] if the world is to be made safe for Democracy. This conflict is indeed a crusade.

Randolph McKim
Sermon, April 6, 1917

We are the Dead. Short days ago
We lived, felt dawn, saw sunset glow,
Loved and were loved, and now we lie,
In Flanders fields.

John McCrea
"In Flanders Fields," *Punch,*1915

■ ■ ■

THE TEENS

(1910–1919)

VOICES OF THE DECADE:
End of Innocence

I think it not improbable that man, like the grub that prepares a chamber for the winged thing it never has seen but is to be— that man may have cosmic destinies he does not understand. And so beyond the vision of battling races and an impoverished earth, I catch a dreaming glimpse of peace.

OLIVER WENDELL HOLMES JR.
Address, Harvard Law Association, February 1913

■ ■ ■

Be patient toward all that is unsolved in your heart.
And try to love the questions themselves.
Do not seek the answers that cannot be given you
because you would not be able to live them.
And the point is to live everything.
Live the questions now.
Perhaps you will then gradually, without noticing it,
live along some distant day into the answer.

RAINER MARIA RILKE
Letters to a Young Poet, 1929

The wise old fairy tales never were so silly as to say that the prince and the princess lived peacefully ever afterwards. The fairy tales said that the prince and the princess lived happily, and so they did. They lived happily, although it is very likely that from time to time they threw the furniture at each other. Most marriages, I think, are happy marriages; but there is no such thing as a contented marriage. The whole pleasure of marriage is that it is a perpetual crisis.

Appreciations and Criticisms of the Works of Charles Dickens, 1911

> O God of earth and altar,
> Bow down and hear our cry,
> Our earthly rulers falter,
> Our people drift and die;
> The walls of gold entomb us,
> The swords of scorn divide,
> Take not thy thunder from us,
> but take away our pride.

G. K. CHESTERTON
"O God of Earth and Altar," *Poems,* 1915

■ ■ ■

Think what it would signify to a local community if all sincere Christian people should interpret their obligation in the social terms which we have been using; if they should not only seek their own salvation, but the reign of God in their own town; if they should cultivate the habit of seeing a divine sacredness in every personality, should assist in creating the economic foundations for fraternal solidarity, and if, as Christians, they should champion the weak in their own community. We need a power of renewal in our American communities that will carry us across the coming social transition, and the social Christianity can supply it by directing the...force of the old faith of our fathers to the new social tasks.

WALTER RAUSCHENBUSCH
The Social Principles of Jesus, 1916

■ ■ ■

FROM THE WORDS OF BILLY SUNDAY

The trouble with many men is that they have got just enough religion to make them miserable. If there is not joy in religion, you have got a leak in your religion.

Sermon, New York City, 1914

■ ■ ■

God likes a little humor, as evidenced by the fact that he made the monkey, the parrot—and some of you people.

Faith is the beginning of something of which you can't see the end but in which you believe.

Going to church doesn't make a man a Christian, any more than going to a garage makes him an automobile.

I tell you with shame, I stretched the elastic bands of my mother's love until I thought they would break. I went far into the dark and the wrong until I ceased to hear her prayers and her pleadings. I forgot her face, and I went so far that it seemed to me that one more step and the elastic bands of her love would break and I would be lost. But, thank God, friends, I never took that last step. Little by little I yielded to the tender memories and recollections of my mother; little by little I was drawn away from the yawning abyss, and...one dark and stormy night in Chicago, I groped my way out of the darkness into the arms of Jesus Christ.

BILLY SUNDAY
Billy Sunday: The Man and His Message, 1917

■ ■ ■

The world stands out on either side
No wider than the heart is wide;
Above the world is stretched the sky,—
No higher than the soul is high.
The heart can push the sea and land
Farther away on either hand;
The soul can split the sky in two,
And let the face of God shine through.
But East and West will pinch the heart
That cannot keep them pushed apart;
And he whose soul is flat—the sky
Will cave in on him by and by.

EDNA ST. VINCENT MILLAY
"Renascence," *Renascence and Other Poems,* 1917

■ ■ ■

The things that Jesus did were of the most menial and commonplace order, and this is an indication that it takes all God's power in me to do the most commonplace things in His way.... All the ordinary sordid things of our lives reveal more quickly than anything what we are made of.

You do not know what you are going to do; the only thing you know is that God knows what He is doing.... It is this attitude that keeps you in perpetual wonder—you do not know what God is going to do next.

OSWALD CHAMBERS
1911–1915 Lectures, *My Utmost for His Highest,* 1935

■ ■ ■

It is not right human thoughts about God that form the content of the Bible, but right divine thoughts about us. The Bible tells us not how we should talk with God, but what God says to us. Not how we find the way to God, but how God has sought and found the way to us.

KARL BARTH
"The Strange New World Within the Bible," 1916

OVERVIEW:

THE TWENTIES

1920–1929   Boom Time

The war was over. The boys were home. Democracy had prevailed over the forces of evil. Now it was time to get back to the business of life in America.

With the twenties modernity reigned: telephones, automobiles, radio, jazz, movies—the promise of ever greater prosperity. The booming economy of the 1920s brought with it a national euphoria, "a kind of swaggering time,"[1] according to Martin Marty. Business tycoons, moneyed magnates, and the rule of Wall Street defined the decade.

The booming economy was also a driving force in the country's religious life. Most of the dates chiseled into cornerstones on the big, old downtown churches and synagogues are from the 1920s (or the 1950s). The twenties was not a time of deep piety. Growth and building were the priorities, and Protestants dominated.

---

1. Martin Marty, *Modern American Religion, Vol. 2, The Noise of Conflict* (Chicago: The University of Chicago Press, 1991), 2–3.

Dr. Marty says, "It was an era of good feelings, but underneath the illusion of well-being was a lot of ugliness. Everybody was mad at everybody. Conflict between peoples...was the most important public religious theme in the period between the two World Wars.... Not since the Civil War [has] America been more torn...in matters specifically religious."

Against this backdrop of cultural conflict, the Roaring Twenties saw the American people reach a level of prosperity and affluence once considered unimaginable. Oil discoveries created boom camps. Women entered the work force in unprecedented numbers. Everyone seemed to have something to celebrate—until Black Thursday, October 24, 1929.

■ ■ ■

The Decade at a Glance

- 1920   Warren G. Harding becomes president.
- 1920   Prohibition begins, ushering in bootleggers, gangsters, and speakeasies.
- 1920   First live radio broadcast airs in Pittsburgh.
- 1920   First blues recording is made by Mamie Smith.
- 1920   The Nineteenth Amendment is ratified, giving women the vote.
- 1921   Race riot in Tulsa sees 50 whites, 200 blacks killed.
- 1921   White Castle, the first fast-food outlet, opens in Kansas City.

- 1921   Congress begins passing laws to restrict immigration.
- 1922   First radio commercial is broadcast, costing $100 for ten minutes.
- 1922   Publication of James Joyce's *Ulysses* is banned in the U.S.
- 1922   Mussolini takes over Italy.
- 1923   Harding dies; Calvin Coolidge becomes president.
- 1924   Coolidge is re-elected.
- 1924   Joseph Stalin dies.
- 1925   The *Scopes* case, called the "Monkey" trial, pits creation against evolution in the first radio-broadcast court case.
- 1925   John Logie Baird invents the television.
- 1926   Ernest Hemingway publishes *The Sun Also Rises,* the same year A. A. Milne publishes *Winnie the Pooh.*
- 1927   *The Jazz Singer,* the first "talking picture," is released.
- 1927   Charles A. Lindbergh becomes the first person to fly across the Atlantic alone.
- 1927   Babe Ruth hits 60 home runs in one season.
- 1928   Herbert Hoover is elected.
- 1928   Sir Alexander Fleming discovers that penicillin destroys bacteria.
- 1928   Amelia Earhart flies across Atlantic.
- 1929   The stock market crashes.
- 1929   The St. Valentine's Day Massacre in Chicago becomes a bloody example of gangster rivalry.

Enduring Moments

Not heroism but healing, not nostrums but normalcy, not revolution but restoration, not agitation but adjustment...not submergence in internationality but sustainment in triumphant nationality.

WARREN G. HARDING
ca 1922

—————

Let me tell you about the very rich. They are different from you and me.

F. SCOTT FITZGERALD
The Rich Boy, 1926

—————

The chief business of the American people is business.

CALVIN COOLIDGE
ca 1925

—————

Adventure is worthwhile in itself.

AMELIA EARHART
ca 1929

—————

In the spring of '27, something bright and alien flashed across the sky. A young Minnesotan who seemed to have had nothing to do with his generation did a heroic thing, and for a moment people set down their glasses in country clubs and speakeasies and thought of their best old dreams.

F. S C O T T F I T Z G E R A L D
referring to Lindbergh's trans-Atlantic flight, ca. 1927

The poets and philosophers before me discovered the unconscious; what I discovered was the scientific method by which the unconscious can be studied.

S I G M U N D F R E U D
Speech, 1926

The world breaks everyone and afterward many are strong at the broken places.

E R N E S T H E M I N G W A Y
A Farewell to Arms, 1929

■ ■ ■

THE TWENTIES

(1920–1929)

VOICES OF THE DECADE:
Boom Time

The love of our neighbor in all its fullness simply means being able to say... "What are you going through?"

SIMONE WEIL
Waiting for God, 1925

■ ■ ■

Some say the world will end in fire,
Some say in ice.
From what I've tasted of desire
I hold with those who favor fire.
But if it had to perish twice,
I think I know enough of hate
To say that for destruction ice
Is also great
And would suffice.

ROBERT FROST
"Fire and Ice," 1923

There is no need to be peculiar in order to find God. The Magi were taught by the heavens to follow a star; and it brought them, not to a paralysing disclosure of the Transcendent, but to a little Boy on His mother's knee.

EVELYN UNDERHILL

The House of the Soul and Concerning the Inner Life, 1926

■ ■ ■

Any religion...is forever in danger of petrification into mere ritual and habit, though ritual and habit be essential to religion.

We know too much, and are convinced of too little. Our literature is a substitute for religion, and so is our religion.

T. S. ELIOT

A Dialogue on Dramatic Poetry, 1928

■ ■ ■

Fundamentalists have at least one characteristic in common with most scientists. Neither can understand that poetic and religious imagination has a way of arriving at truth by giving a clue to the total meaning of things without being in any sense an analytic description of detailed facts. The fundamentalists insist that religion is science, and thus they prompt those who know that this is not true to declare that all religious truth is contrary to scientific fact.

How can an age which is so devoid of poetic imagination as ours be truly religious?

REINHOLD NIEBUHR
Leaves from the Notebook of a Tamed Cynic, 1929

■ ■ ■

The most secret, sacred wish that lies deep down at the bottom of your heart, the wonderful thing that you hardly dare to look at, or to think about—the thing that you would rather die than have anyone else know of, because it seems so far beyond anything that you are, or have at the present time, that you fear that you would be cruelly ridiculed if the mere thought of it were known—that is just the very thing that God is wishing you to do or to be for him. And the birth of that marvelous wish in your soul—the dawning of that secret dream—was the Voice of God himself telling you to arise and come up higher because he had need of you.

EMMET FOX
Your Heart's Desire, ca. 1922

■ ■ ■

I believe that life is given us so we may grow in love, and I believe that God is in me as the sun is in the colour and fragrance of a flower—the Light in my darkness, the Voice in my silence.

I believe that only in broken gleams has the Sun of Truth yet shone upon men. I believe that love will finally establish the Kingdom of God on earth, and that the Cornerstones of that Kingdom will be Liberty, Truth, Brotherhood, and Service.

I believe that no good shall be lost, and that all man has willed or hoped or dreamed of good shall exist forever.

I believe in the immortality of the soul because I have within me immortal longings.... I believe that in the life to come I shall have the senses I have not had here, and that my home there will be beautiful with colour, music, and speech of flowers and faces I love.

Without this faith there would be little meaning in my life. I should be "a mere pillar of darkness in the dark." Observers in the full enjoyment of their bodily senses pity me, but it is because they do not see the golden chamber in my life where I dwell delighted; for, dark as my path may seem to them, I carry a magic light in my heart. Faith, the spiritual strong searchlight, illumines the way, and although sinister doubts may lurk in the shadow, I walk unafraid towards the Enchanted Wood where the foliage is always green, where joy abides, where nightingales nest and sing, and where life and death are one in the Presence of the Lord.

HELEN KELLER
Midstream, 1929

■   ■   ■

O Lord, we come this morning
Knee-bowed and body-bent
Before thy throne of grace.
O Lord—this morning—
Bow our hearts beneath our knees,
And our knees in some lonesome valley.
We come this morning—
Like empty pitchers to a full fountain,
With no merits of our own.
O Lord—open up a window of heaven,
And lean out far over the battlements of glory,
And listen this morning....

JAMES WELDON JOHNSON
"Listen, Lord—A Prayer," *God's Trombones,* 1927

■   ■   ■

The Skin Horse had lived longer in the nursery than any of the others. He was so old that his brown coat was bald in patches and showed the seams underneath, and most of the hairs in his tail had been pulled out to string bead necklaces. He was wise, for he had seen a long succession of mechanical toys arrive to boast and swagger, and by-and-by break their mainsprings and pass away....

"What is REAL?" asked the Rabbit one day, when they were lying side by side near the nursery fender, before Nana came to tidy the room. "Does it mean having things that buzz inside you and a stick-out handle?"

"Real isn't how you are made," said the Skin Horse. "It's a thing that happens to you. When a child loves you for a long, long time, not just to play with, but REALLY loves you, then you become Real."

"Does it hurt?" asked the Rabbit.

"Sometimes," said the Skin Horse, for he was always truthful. "When you are REAL you don't mind being hurt."

"Does it happen all at once, like being wound up," he asked, "or bit by bit?"

"It doesn't happen all at once," said the Skin Horse. "You become. It takes a long time. That's why it doesn't often happen to people who break easily, or have sharp edges, or who have to be carefully kept. Generally, by the time you are Real, most of your hair has been loved off, and your eyes drop out and you get loose in the joints and very shabby. But these things don't matter at all, because once you are Real you can't be ugly, except to people who don't understand."

MARGERY WILLIAMS
The Velveteen Rabbit, 1922

OVERVIEW:

THE THIRTIES

1930–1939   After the Crash

The thirties brought something Americans had never known on so vast a scale—poverty, panic, fear, and deprivation. The Great Depression changed forever the generation that would give birth to the baby boomers and defined what it meant to survive hard times. It was pervasive, unrelenting, nationwide. From the urban sophistication of Wall Street to the heartland of rural America, the depression showed no mercy, no favoritism.

The Stock Market Crash of 1929, the collapse of the U.S. banking system in 1933, and the severe drought that turned the Great Plains into a dust bowl threw the United States into economic chaos. Thousands of suicides were reported in the months following the crash. Desperate farmers dumped gallons of milk to try to drive up prices, but farm income still dropped by 50 percent. In addition, industry production was reduced by half, 85,000 businesses failed, numerous banks closed, and unemployment reached 25 percent.

Religious bickering paled against the harshness of drought,

unemployment, starvation, and hardship. Against that back-drop, the theological mood of the country shifted, and a new type of theologian emerged. These thinkers, including American-born brothers H. Richard and Reinhold Niebuhr, and immigrant Paul Tillich, "aspired to be public theologians.... They employed the language of faith to address a public also beyond the churches. They...functioned almost as novelists or artists do," writes Dr. Marty.[2]

The querulous noise of cultural conflict of the twenties was silenced by the hard realities of the thirties. Singing telegrams and the music of Benny Goodman couldn't soften life for the 40 million people living in poverty or the thousands of workers out on strikes. After the crash, Americans were suffering.

■ ■ ■

The Decade at a Glance

- • 1930   Grant Wood exhibits *American Gothic.*
- • 1931   The Empire State Building opens in New York.
- • 1931   Al Capone is jailed for income tax evasion.
- • 1932   America is stunned as headlines report kidnapping of the Lindbergh baby.

2. Martin Marty, *Modern American Religion. Vol. 2, The Noise of Conflict* (Chicago: The University of Chicago Press, 1991), 306.

- 1932 Shirley Temple's first movie is released.
- 1933 Franklin Delano Roosevelt is inaugurated and launches The New Deal, an unprecedented number of emergency relief and recovery programs.
- 1933 Passing of Twenty-first Amendment repeals Prohibition.
- 1933 Hitler becomes chancellor of Germany.
- 1934 Federal law grants labor the right to form unions, but strong-arm tactics stall unionization.
- 1934 Walt Disney releases *Snow White,* America's first full-length animated movie.
- 1935 Social Security Act instituted.
- 1936 Edward VIII of Great Britain abdicates the throne to marry American Wallis Simpson.
- 1936 Jesse Owens captures four gold medals at the Berlin Olympics.
- 1937 First jet engine is built.
- 1938 Orson Welles' radio broadcast of *War of the Worlds* on Halloween night creates a nationwide hysteria.
- 1938 Fair Labor Standards Act is passed, limiting child labor.
- 1939 War breaks out in Europe, a war that from its first day was called World War II.
- 1939 John Steinbeck publishes *The Grapes of Wrath.*
- 1939 An atom is split by John Dunning at Columbia University.

■   ■   ■

Enduring Moments

Once I built a railroad,

now it's done.

Brother, can you spare a dime?

EDGAR Y. HARBURG AND JAY GORNEY
"Brother, Can You Spare a Dime?," 1932

Certainly there are lots of things in life that

money won't buy, but it's very funny—

Have you ever tried to buy them without money?

OGDEN NASH
"The Terrible People," *Happy Days,* 1933

Only to the white man was nature a "wilderness."

LUTHER STANDING BEAR
Land of the Spotted Eagle, 1933

While I can make no claim for having introduced the term "rugged individualism," I should be proud to have invented it.

HERBERT HOOVER
The Challenge to Liberty, 1934

We'll be the first nation in the history of the world to go to the poor house in an automobile.

WILL ROGERS
ca. 1933

A change has come over the spirit of our times, and the old faiths and hopes no longer carry convictions, when stated in the old terms.

WALTER MARSHALL HORTON
Realistic Theology, 1934

I have found it impossible to carry the heavy burden of responsibility and to discharge my duties as King...without the help and support of the woman I love.

EDWARD VIII
Radio address, December 11, 1936

Some recent work...which has been communicated to me in manuscript, leads me to expect that the element uranium may be turned into a new and important source of energy in the immediate future.

ALBERT EINSTEIN
Letter to Franklin D. Roosevelt, August 2, 1939

THE THIRTIES

(1930–1939)

VOICES OF THE DECADE:
After the Crash

The door opened and he stood there, fresh-skinned and glowing. There was something about his eyes. He was inexplicably different. What had happened?

I pushed a drink across the table. He refused it. Disappointed but curious, I wondered what had got into the fellow. He wasn't himself.

"Come, what's this all about?" I queried.

He looked straight at me. Simply, but smilingly, he said, "I've got religion."

I was aghast. So that was it—last summer an alcoholic crackpot; now, I suspected, a little cracked about religion. He had that starry-eyed look. Yes, the old boy was on fire all right. But bless his heart, let him rant! Beside, my gin would last longer than his preaching.

But he did no ranting. In a matter of fact way he told how two men had appeared in court, persuading the judge to suspend his commitment. They had told of a simple religious idea and a practical program of action. That was two months ago and the result was self-evident. It worked!

He had come to pass his experience along to me—if I cared to have it. I was shocked, but interested. I had to be, for I was hopeless....

I had always believed in a Power greater than myself. I had often pondered these things. I was not an atheist. Few people really are....

To Christ I conceded the certainty of a great man, not too closely followed by those who claimed Him. His moral teaching—most excellent. For myself, I had adopted those parts which seemed convenient and not too difficult; the rest I disregarded.... I honestly doubted whether, on balance, the religions of mankind had done any good. Judging from what I had seen in Europe and since, the power of God in human affairs was negligible, the Brotherhood of Man a grim jest. If there was a Devil, he seemed the Boss Universal, and he certainly had me.

But my friend sat before me, and he made the pointblank declaration that God had done for him what he could not do for himself.... Here was something at work in a human heart which had done the impossible. My ideas about miracles were drastically revised right then....

There I humbly offered myself to God, as I then understood

Him, to do with me as He would. I placed myself unreservedly under His care and direction. I admitted for the first time that of myself I was nothing; that without Him I was lost. I ruthlessly faced my sins and became willing to have my new-found Friend take them away, root and branch. I have not had a drink since....

God comes to most men gradually, but his impact on me was sudden and profound.

BILL W.
Alcoholics Anonymous, 1934

■ ■ ■

Religion at its best has supplied—and it can now supply—convictions by which men inwardly come to terms with themselves, gain spiritual peace and power, and come off more than conquerors.

HARRY EMERSON FOSDICK
Adventurous Religion, 1926

■ ■ ■

If we want to know what happiness is we must seek it, not as if it were a pot of gold at the end of the rainbow, but among human beings who are living richly and fully the good life. If you observe a really happy man you will find him building a boat, writing a symphony, educating his son, growing double dahlias in his garden. He will not be searching for happiness as if it were a collar button that has rolled under the radiator. He will have become aware that he is happy in the course of living twenty-four crowded hours of the day....

To find happiness we must seek for it in a focus outside ourselves....

No one has learned the meaning of living until he has surrendered his ego to the service of his fellow-men.

W. BERAN WOLFE
How to Be Happy Though Human, 1931

■ ■ ■

My spiritual life is not something specialised and intense; a fenced-off devotional patch rather difficult to cultivate, and needing to be sheltered from the cold winds of the outer world. Nor is it an alternative to my outward, practical life. On the contrary, it is the very source of that quality and purpose which makes my practical life worth while.

Many people seem to think that the spiritual life necessarily requires a definite and exacting plan of study; it does not. But it does require a definite plan of life; and courage in sticking to the plan, not merely for days or weeks, but for years.... This is something which cannot be hurried; but, unless we take it seriously, can be infinitely delayed. Many people suggest by their behaviour that God is of far less importance than their bath, morning paper, or early cup of tea.

EVELYN UNDERHILL
The Spiritual Life, 1937

■ ■ ■

Life is meant to be lived from a Center, a divine Center.... There is a divine Abyss within us all, a holy Infinite Center, a Heart, a Life who speaks in us and through us to the world. We have all heard this holy Whisper at times. At times we have followed the Whisper, an amazing equilibrium of life, amazing effectiveness of living set in. But too many of us have heeded the Voice only at times.... We have not counted this Holy Thing within us to be the most precious thing in the world.

THOMAS R. KELLY
A Testament of Devotion, 1941

■ ■ ■

Love and ever more love is the only solution to every problem that comes up. If we love each other enough, we will bear with each other's faults and burdens. If we love enough, we are going to light that fire in the hearts of others. And it is love that will burn out the sins and hatreds that sadden us. It is love that will make us want to do great things for each other. No sacrifice and no suffering will then seem too much.

Yes, I see only too clearly how bad people are. I wish I did not see it so. It is my own sins that give me such clarity.

DOROTHY DAY
"House of Hospitality," ca 1930

■ ■ ■

Has any spiritual fabric ever been built except upon invisible foundations? "The steps of faith fall on the seeming void and find the rock beneath"; but the rock is hardly ever seen till afterwards. Just when the step has to be taken, coils of blinding, smothering mist descend upon the path.... And the foot that seems to step out on nothing finds rock.

AMY CARMICHAEL
Gold Cord, 1932

■ ■ ■

All men who live with any degree of serenity live by some assurance of grace.

REINHOLD NIEBUHR
Reflections on the End of an Era, 1934

■　■　■

Today is a new day. You will get out of it just what you put into it. If you have made mistakes, even serious mistakes, there is always another chance for you. And supposing you have tried and failed again and again, you may have a fresh start any moment you choose, for this thing that we call "failure" is not the falling down, but the staying down.

MARY PICKFORD
Why Not Try God?, 1934

■　■　■

Men do not stand, one by one, like bottles in the rain, rather like interflowing streams, they share their fortunes.

HARRY EMERSON FOSDICK
A Guide to Understanding the Bible, 1938

■　■　■

The conviction came that that rhythm was too orderly, too harmonious, too perfect to be a product of blind chance—that, therefore, there must be purpose in the whole and that man was part of that whole and not an accidental offshoot. It was a feeling that transcended reason; that went to the heart of a man's despair and found it groundless.

RICHARD E. BYRD
Alone, 1938

OVERVIEW:

THE FORTIES

1940–1949   A Heroic Effort

O ne returns from Europe with the sound of weeping in one's ears…. An awful solemnity is upon the earth," wrote Quaker Thomas R. Kelly in 1938. His words were prophetic: an awful solemnity was indeed upon the earth. Called the "last good war," World War II brought a unified mobilization in American history unparalleled before or since.

Franklin Delano Roosevelt and Harry S Truman are names synonymous with a country in crisis, a country recovering from the worst economic era in its history, a country prepared to meet a global threat.

Events between the years 1940 and 1949 *not* related to the war are seldom reflected in the stories retold from one genera-tion to another. A few non-war remembrances have survived, like the jitterbug, the zoot suit, and the transistor. This decade also marked the birth of McDonalds, the LP (long-play record), the zoom lens, and the term "weekend." But the most well-known descriptors of the decade reveal the impact of the war: war rations, war bride, Rosie the Riveter, and the hit song,

"Boogie Woogie Bugle Boy of Company B." This was the decade of gas rationing, G.I. Joes, and Bob Hope's Goodwill USO Tours. Poster pin-ups with the memorable images of Betty Grable and Rita Hayworth shored up the morale of boys far from home.

When the war ended the veterans who had fought the good fight with uncompromising resolve, determination, and grit directed those same qualities toward building the good life at home. These were men and women with a mission, determined to live life to the fullest—to justify the hand of fate that spared their lives while taking the lives of so many with whom they had fought. The national goal and pastime became, as one naval petty officer said, "Raise babies and keep house!"

■ ■ ■

The Decade at a Glance

- 1940   Selective Service Act is passed, the first peacetime draft in American history
- 1940   Franklin Delano Roosevelt wins third term.
- 1941   The first "regular" television broadcasting begins in New York City.
- 1941   The Japanese attack Pearl Harbor, killing 2,300 Americans, and drawing the United States into World War II.

- 1942   Humphrey Bogart and Ingrid Bergman star in *Casablanca*.
- 1942   Americans of Japanese ancestry are sent to "relocation" camps.
- 1944   Allies begin D-Day invasion of Europe.
- 1944   Congress passes the GI Bill, offering government aid to veterans for housing, education, and business.
- 1944   Billy Graham holds his first rally in May at the 3,000-seat Orchestra Hall in Chicago; by October he fills the 30,000-seat Chicago Stadium.
- 1944   Harvard develops the first computer, Mark I.
- 1944   Roosevelt elected to fourth term.
- 1945   Roosevelt dies and Harry S Truman is sworn in.
- 1945   The United States drops atomic bombs on Hiroshima and Nagasaki to end the war.
- 1946   Jimmy Stewart stars in *It's a Wonderful Life*.
- 1947   Chuck Yeager breaks the sound barrier.
- 1947   Jackie Robinson signs on with the Brooklyn Dodgers, becoming the first black baseball player in the major leagues.
- 1947   The Cold War begins between the Soviet Union and the United States.
- 1948   The first bikinis show up on American beaches.
- 1948   Mohandas K. Gandhi is assassinated in India.
- 1948   The state of Israel is established.
- 1948   Truman defeats Dewey for president.
- 1949   George Orwell publishes *1984*.
- 1949   NATO is formed.

Enduring Moments

I have nothing to offer but blood, toil, tears, and sweat.

WINSTON CHURCHILL
Inaugural address, May 13, 1940

In the nightmare of the dark

All the dogs of Europe bark,

And the living nations wait,

Each sequestered in its hate....

W. H. AUDEN
"In Memory of W. B. Yeats," 1940

Don't sit under the apple tree with anyone else but me....

LEW BROWN, CHARLIE TOBIAS, AND

SAM H. STEPT
"Don't Sit Under the Apple Tree," 1942

More than an end to war, we want an end to the beginnings of all wars.

FRANKLIN DELANO ROOSEVELT
1945

My God, what have we done?

ROBERT LEWIS
Copilot of the *Enola Gay*, after dropping atom bomb, 1945

The more people have studied different methods of bringing up children the more they have come to the conclusion that what good mothers and fathers instinctively feel like doing for their babies is the best after all.

BENJAMIN SPOCK
The Common Sense Book of Baby and Child Care, 1946

There are those who say to you—we are rushing this issue of civil rights. I say we are 172 years late.

HUBERT H. HUMPHREY
Address, Democratic National Convention, July 14, 1948

[Television] won't be able to hold on to any market it captures after the first six months. People will soon get tired of staring at a plywood box every night.

DARRYL F. ZANUCK
ca. 1949

■ ■ ■

THE FORTIES

(1940–1949)

VOICES OF THE DECADE:
A Heroic Effort

In the future days, which we seek to make secure, we look forward to a world founded upon four essential human freedoms. The first is freedom of speech and expression—everywhere in the world. The second is freedom of every person to worship God in his own way—everywhere in the world. The third is freedom from want—everywhere in the world. The fourth is freedom from fear—which, translated into world terms, means a worldwide reduction of armaments to such a point and in such a thorough fashion that no nation will be in a position to commit an act of physical aggression against any neighbor—anywhere in the world.

FRANKLIN DELANO ROOSEVELT
Congressional address, January 6, 1941

■　■　■

Prayer is a force as real as terrestrial gravity. As a physician, I have seen men, after all other therapy has failed, lifted out of disease and melancholy by the serene effort of prayer. It is the only power in the world that seems to overcome the so-called "laws of nature"; the occasions on which prayer has dramatically done this have been termed "miracles." But a constant, quieter miracle takes place hourly in the hearts of men and women who have discovered that prayer supplies them with a steady flow of sustaining power in their daily lives.

Too many people regard prayer as a formalized routine of words, a refuge for weaklings, or a childish petition for material things. We sadly undervalue prayer when we conceive it in these terms, just as we should underestimate rain by describing it as something that fills the birdbath in our garden. Properly understood, prayer is a mature activity indispensable to the fullest development of personality—the ultimate integration of man's highest faculties. Only in prayer do we achieve that complete and harmonious assembly of body, mind, and spirit which gives the frail human reed its unshakable strength.

ALEXIS CARREL
"Prayer Is Power," *The Reader's Digest,* March 1941

■ ■ ■

FROM THE WRITINGS OF C. S. LEWIS

A man who was merely a man and said the sort of things Jesus said would not be a great moral teacher. He would either be a lunatic—on a level with the man who says he is a poached egg...or else a madman or something worse.... Now it seems to me obvious that He was neither a lunatic nor a fiend: and consequently, however strange or terrifying or unlikely it may seem, I have to accept the view that He was and is God.

Doctrines are not God: they are only a kind of map. But that map is based on the experience of hundreds of people who really were in touch with God—experiences compared with which any thrills or pious feelings you and I are likely to get on our own are very elementary and very confused.... If you want to get any further, you must use the map... That is just why a vague religion—all about feeling God in nature, and so on—is so attractive. It is all thrills and no work; like watching the waves from the beach. But you will not get to Newfoundland by studying the Atlantic that way, and you will not get eternal life by simply feeling the presence of God in flowers or music. Neither will you get anywhere by looking at maps without going to sea. Nor will you be very safe if you go to sea without a map.

In other words, theology is practical.... If you do not listen to theology, that will not mean that you have no ideas about God. It will mean that you have a lot of wrong ones—bad, muddled, out-of-date ideas. For a great many of the ideas about God which are trotted out as novelties today, are simply the ones which real theologians tried centuries ago and rejected.

Aim at Heaven and you will get earth "thrown in": aim at earth and you will get neither.

C. S. LEWIS
Mere Christianity, 1943

■ ■ ■

Perhaps it is no wonder that the women were first at the Cradle and last at the Cross. They had never known a man like this Man—there never has been such another. A prophet and teacher who never nagged at them, never flattered or coaxed or patronized; who never made arch jokes about them, never treated them either as "The women, God help us!" or "The ladies, God bless them!"; who rebuked without querulousness and praised without condescension; who took their questions and arguments seriously; who never mapped out their sphere for them, never urged them to be feminine or jeered at them for being female; who had no axe to grind and no uneasy male dignity to defend; who took them as he found them and was completely unself-conscious. There is no act, no sermon, no parable in the whole Gospel that borrows its pungency from female perversity; nobody could possibly guess from the words and deeds of Jesus that there was anything "funny" about woman's nature.

DOROTHY SAYERS
Unpopular Opinions, 1947

The more faithfully you listen to the voice within you,
the better you will hear what is sounding outside.

DAG HAMMARSKJÖLD
1942 diary entry, *Markings,* 1964

■ ■ ■

We shall not cease from exploration
And the end of all our exploring
Will be to arrive where we started
And know the place for the first time.

T. S. ELIOT
"Little Gidding," 1942

■ ■ ■

FROM THE WRITINGS OF DIETRICH BONHOEFFER

We must be ready to allow ourselves to be interrupted by God...
We must not...assume that our schedule is our own to manage,
but allow it to be arranged by God.

Cost of Discipleship, 1937

How wrong it is to use God as a stop-gap for the incompleteness
of our knowledge.... We are to find God in what we know, not
in what we don't know; God wants us to realize his presence, not
in unsolved problems but in those that are solved.... God is no

stop-gap; he must be recognized as the centre of life, not when we are at the end of our resources.

I believe that nothing that happens to me is meaningless, and that it is good for us all that it should be so, even if it runs counter to our own wishes. As I see it, I'm here for some purpose, and I only hope I may fulfil it. In the light of the great purpose all our privations and disappointments are trivial.

DIETRICH BONHOEFFER
Letters and Papers From Prison, 1943–1944

Compilers' Note: *Dietrich Bonhoeffer was a German pastor, teacher, and theologian who actively resisted the Nazi rise to power in pre–World War II Germany. On April 5, 1943, he was arrested and imprisoned. Two years later, on April 9, 1945, shortly before the concentration camp at Flossenburg was liberated by Allied forces, Dietrich Bonhoeffer was executed by special order of Heinrich Himmler. He was 39 years old.*

■ ■ ■

We who lived in concentration camps can remember the men who walked through the huts comforting others, giving away their last piece of bread. They may have been few in number, but they offer sufficient proof that everything can be taken from a man but one thing: the last of the human freedoms—to choose one's attitude in any given set of circumstances, to choose one's own way.

And there were always choices to make. Every day, every hour, offered the opportunity to make a decision, a decision which determined whether you would or would not submit to those powers which threatened to rob you of your very self, your inner freedom; which determined whether or not you would become the plaything of circumstance, renouncing freedom and dignity to become molded into the form of the typical inmate.

Fundamentally, therefore, any man can, even under such circumstances, decide what shall become of him—mentally and spiritually. He may retain his human dignity even in a concentration camp. Dostoevski said once, "There is only one thing that I dread: not to be worthy of my sufferings." These words frequently came to my mind after I became acquainted with those martyrs whose behavior in camp, whose suffering and death, bore witness to the fact that the last inner freedom cannot be lost.

VIKTOR E. FRANKL
Man's Search for Meaning, 1959

■ ■ ■

God, grant me the serenity to accept the things I cannot change;

      courage to change the things I can;

      and the wisdom to know the difference.

Living one day at a time;

      enjoying one moment at a time.

      accepting hardship as the pathway to peace;

Taking, as He did, this sinful world as it is, not as I would have it;

      Trusting that He will make all things right,

      if I surrender to His will;

      That I may be reasonably happy in this life,

      and supremely happy with Him forever in the next.

      Amen.

REINHOLD NIEBUHR
"The Serenity Prayer," ca 1944

■ ■ ■

No one can get inner peace by pouncing on it, by vigorously willing to have it. Peace is a margin of power around our daily need. Peace is a consciousness of springs too deep for earthly droughts to dry up. Peace is an awareness of reserves from beyond ourselves, so that our power is not so much in us as through us.

HARRY EMERSON FOSDICK
Radio address, January 6, 1946

■ ■ ■

Many souls fail to find God because they want a religion which will remake society without remaking themselves.

FULTON J. SHEEN
Peace of Soul, 1949

■ ■ ■

If God is present at every point in space, if we cannot go where He is not, cannot even conceive of a place where is He is not, why then has not that Presence become the one universally celebrated fact of the world? The patriarch Jacob, "in waste howling wilderness," gave the answer to that question. He saw a vision of God and cried out in wonder, "Surely the Lord is in this place; and I knew it not." Jacob had never been for one small division of a moment outside the circle of that all-pervading Presence. But he knew it not. That was his trouble, and it is ours. Men do not know if God is here. What a difference it would make if they knew.

A. W. TOZER
The Pursuit of God, 1948

■ ■ ■

O Lord, our God, have pity upon us,
who have so little pity in our hearts.
We give, but not in kindness.

We give because the sound of crying disturbs us....

O Lord, be patient with us.

Give us yet more time to learn what love is,

and how love should act,

and how love can change us as individuals and as a nation.

We pray in the name of Him who loves us all.

U.S. Senate Chaplain, Prayer, May 26, 1948

Where we cannot convince,

let us be willing to persuade,

for small deeds done are better than great deeds planned.

We know that we cannot do everything.

But help us to do something.

For Jesus' sake. Amen.

PETER MARSHALL
U.S. Senate Chaplain, Prayer, January 27, 1949

Compilers' Note: *According to Catherine Marshall's book,* The Prayers of Peter Marshall, *soon after accepting the position of Chaplain to the U.S. Senate, Peter Marshall commented, "It's quite obvious that the Senators appreciate my prayers in inverse ratio to their length." Dr. Marshall had already written this prayer for the opening of the Senate for January 27, 1949. Before his untimely death on January 25, en route to the hospital, he asked that the prayer be read for the Senate opening.*

O Holy Spirit of God, visit now this soul of mine, and tarry within it until eventide. Inspire all my thoughts. Pervade all my imaginations. Suggest all my decisions.... Be with me in my silence and in my speech, in my haste and in my leisure, in company and in solitude, in the freshness of the morning and in the weariness of the evening; and give me grace at all times to rejoice in thy mysterious companionship.

JOHN BAILLIE
A Diary of Private Prayer, 1949

Overview:

The Fifties

1950–1959   The American Dream

Ozzie and Harriett. Lucy and Desi. Buddy Holly, Ritchie Valens, the Big Bopper, and Elvis Presley. For the first time in our history, cultural icons were those created and sustained by mass media and mass marketing. To say "the fifties" is to invoke the sound of rock 'n roll or the image of Lucy and her sidekick Ethel stomping grapes with their bare feet. For many Americans, these were happy days, well deserving of the nostalgia they evoke.

"Looking at the whole of American history, this is the decade when everything worked," Marty says.

The pursuit of the American dream led to the beginning of the Space Age, satellite technology, and a renewed vision of uncharted frontiers. Words like *beatnik* and *DNA* entered the vocabulary.

The fifties brought the development of suburbia. Housing, schools, and city and state services experienced dramatic growth as the first wave of baby boomers started school. Bicycle production increased 90 percent. Little League participation rose more than 600 percent, and Girl Scout membership saw a 122 percent increase. The ex-GIs returning home, marrying, moving to the suburbs, and raising families exemplified social conformity, but not all segments of society fared so well.

In American religion, this was the strongest decade according to every indicator: gifts, membership, contributions, volunteering, and church building. Identity was determined by religious affiliation; going to church was a given. With the growth of suburbs, long-standing barriers between religious groups began to crumble as Polish Catholics lived next door to Swedish Lutherans who lived just down the street from a Jewish synagogue. Even in an age of social conformity, ecumenism was born.

■ ■ ■

The Decade at a Glance

- 1950   Senator Joseph McCarthy embarks on a public crusade to uncover Communist activity in the U.S.
- 1950   First kidney transplant and first successful heart massage are performed.
- 1950   U.S. sends troops to Korea.
- 1951   Color television is introduced.
- 1952   A priest, minister, and rabbi sanction the appearance of Lucille Ball's pregnancy on her TV show.
- 1952   Albert Schweitzer is awarded the Nobel Peace Prize.
- 1952   President Dwight D. Eisenhower is elected.

- 1953   Jonas Salk's polio vaccine is certified to prevent infantile paralysis.
- 1954   Congress adds the phrase "under God" to the Pledge of Allegiance.
- 1954   *Brown v The Board of Education of Topeka, Kansas* outlaws segregation in schools striking down the doctrine of "separate but equal."
- 1955   Rosa Parks refuses to give up her seat on a city bus and, in effect, begins the civil rights movement.
- 1956   Elvis Presley releases "Heartbreak Hotel" and starts a music revolution.
- 1956   Eisenhower and Nixon win again.
- 1957   Federal troops are called in to protect the Little Rock Nine, the first black students to attend all-white Central High.
- 1957   The baby boom peaks at 4.3 million births.
- 1957   The USSR launches a satellite, *Sputnik I,* into orbit around the earth.
- 1959   The first Barbie doll is introduced.
- 1959   Texas Instruments invents the microchip.
- 1959   Alaska becomes the 49th state, Hawaii the 50th.

■   ■   ■

Enduring Moments

I have in my hand a list of two hundred and five [people] that were known to the Secretary of State as being members of the Communist Party.

JOSEPH MCCARTHY
Speech, February 9, 1950

If the television craze continues with the present level of programs, we are destined to have a nation of morons.

DANIEL MARSH
President of Boston College, *Columbia Chronicles,* 1950

Don't look back. Something might be gaining on you.

SATCHEL PAIGE
Black American baseball player, 1953

Roll over Beethoven. And tell Tchaikovsky the news.

CHUCK BERRY
"Roll Over Beethoven," 1956

We conclude that in the field of education the doctrine of "separate but equal" has no place.

Earl Warren
Chief Justice, *Brown v. The Board of Education,* 1954

Recognition of the Supreme Being is the first, the most basic, expression of Americanism. Without God, there could be no American form of government, nor American way of life.

Dwight D. Eisenhower
American Chronicle, 1955

Work expands so as to fill the time available for its completion.

Cyril Northcote Parkinson
Parkinson's Law, 1957

Unless we get off our fat surpluses and recognize that television in the main is being used to distract, delude, amuse, and insulate us, then television and those who finance it, those who look at it and those who work at it, may see a totally different picture too late.

Edward R. Murrow

ca 1958

■ ■ ■

THE FIFTIES

(1950–1959)

Science without religion is lame, religion without science is blind.

ALBERT EINSTEIN
Out of My Later Years, 1950

■ ■ ■

Often God has to shut a door in our face, so that He can subsequently open the door through which He wants us to go.

CATHERINE MARSHALL
A Man Called Peter, 1951

■ ■ ■

Through the high jungle tree tops, the news quickly spread:
He talks to a dust speck! He's out of his head!
Just look at him walk with that speck on that flower!
And Horton walked, worrying, almost an hour.
"Should I put this speck down?" Horton thought with alarm.
"If I do, these small persons may come to great harm.

I can't put it down. And I won't! After all
A person's a person. No matter how small."

DR. SEUSS (THEODOR SEUSS GEISEL)
Horton Hears a Who, 1954

■ ■ ■

FROM THE JOURNALS OF DAG HAMMARSKJÖLD

No peace which is not peace for all, no rest until all has been
fulfilled.

Never, "for the sake of peace and quiet," deny your own experience or convictions.

Your prayer has been answered, as you know. God has a use for
you, even though what He asks doesn't happen to suit you at
the moment.

We are not permitted to choose the frame of our destiny. But
what we put into it is ours. He who wills adventure will experience it—according to the measure of his courage.

God does not die on the day when we cease to believe in a personal deity, but we die on the day when our lives cease to be

illumined by the steady radiance, renewed daily of a wonder, the source of which is beyond all reason.

DAG HAMMARSKJÖLD
1950–53 diary entries, *Markings,* 1964

■ ■ ■

FROM THE PREACHING OF
GEORGE A. BUTTRICK

For whatever high reasons, men of prayer must knock and knock and knock—sometimes with bleeding knuckles in the dark.

It appears that when life is broken by tragedy God shines through the breach.

Prayer, 1942

Sin is poison poured into the stream of time.

Sermons Preached in a University Church, 1959

The Bible reveals our brokenness while bringing persuasions of grace. Generation by generation men find there a lamp for their feet and a light on their path. Otherwise they stumble in darkness.

GEORGE A. BUTTRICK
Interpreter's Dictionary of the Bible, 1962

■　■　■

Grace creates liberated laughter. The grace of God in Jesus Christ is beautiful, and it radiates joy and awakens humor.

KARL BARTH
Church Dogmatics, vol. II, part 1, 1957

■　■　■

To believe in something not yet proved and to underwrite it with our lives; it is the only way we can leave the future open. Man, surrounded by facts, permitting himself no surprise, no intuitive flash, no great hypothesis, no risk, is in a locked cell. Ignorance cannot seal the mind and imagination more securely.

LILLIAN SMITH
The Journey, 1954

■　■　■

He is the Way
Follow Him through the Land of Unlikeness;
You will see rare beasts, and have unique adventures.

He is the Truth.
Seek Him in the Kingdom of Anxiety;
You will come to a great city that has expected
　　your return for years.

He is the Life.

Love Him in the World of the Flesh;

And at your marriage all its occasions shall dance for joy.

W. H. AUDEN
For the Time Being: A Christmas Oratorio in Religious Drama 1, 1957

■ ■ ■

I want first of all...to be at peace with myself. I want a singleness of eye, a purity of intention, a central core to my life that will enable me to carry out these obligations and activities as well as I can. I want, in fact—to borrow from the language of the saints—to live "in grace" as much of the time as possible. I am not using this term in a strictly theological sense. By grace I mean an inner harmony, essentially spiritual, which can be translated into outward harmony. I am seeking perhaps what Socrates asked for..."May the outward and inward man be at one."

With a new awareness, both painful and humorous, I begin to understand why the saints were rarely married women. I am convinced it has nothing to do, as I once supposed, with chastity or children. It has to do primarily with distractions.

ANNE MORROW LINDBERGH
Gift from the Sea, 1955

■ ■ ■

We can never live in the past as if it were our true home.... And it is a good thing that God draws this veil over the past even without our asking. In so doing, He allows us to live to-day for to-morrow with just the few memories we need of what was.

KARL BARTH
Church Dogmatics, vol. III, part 2, 1960

■　■　■

The spiritual life is first of all a life.

It is not merely something to be known and studied, it is to be lived. Like all life, it grows sick and dies when it is uprooted from its proper element.... We live as spiritual [people] when we live as [people] seeking God. If we are to become spiritual, we must remain [human]. And if there were not evidence of this everywhere in theology, the Mystery of the Incarnation itself would be ample proof of it.... Jesus lived the ordinary life of the men of His time, in order to sanctify the ordinary lives of men of all time. If we want to be spiritual, then, let us first of all live our lives. Let us not fear the responsibilities and the inevitable distractions of the work appointed for us by the will of God. Let us embrace reality and thus find ourselves immersed in the life-giving will and wisdom of God which surrounds us everywhere.

THOMAS MERTON
Thoughts in Solitude, 1956

I am no disbeliever in spiritual purpose and no vague believer. I see from the standpoint of Christian orthodoxy. This means for me the meaning of life is centered in our Redemption by Christ and that what I see in the world I see in relation to that.

Redemption is meaningless unless there is cause for it in the actual life we live, and for the last few centuries there has been operating in our culture the secular belief that there is no such cause.

FLANNERY O'CONNOR
"The Fiction Writer and His Country," *The Living Novel: A Symposium*

■ ■ ■

Being religious means asking passionately the question of the meaning of our existence and being willing to receive answers, even if the answers hurt.

PAUL TILLICH
The Saturday Evening Post, June 14, 1958

■ ■ ■

So deep and meaningful is the joy and the enthusiasm that is born in one's mind and heart by human love and helpfulness that it has the power to motivate for a lifetime....

You don't have to be a doctor to say or do that which puts light in a human eye and joy on a human face. Simply practice

Jesus' commandment that we love one another. Go out and do something for somebody. These are the things that make happy people. Here is the one never-failing source of the joy and enthusiasm we are talking about.

NORMAN VINCENT PEALE
Treasury of Joy and Enthusiasm, 1981

■ ■ ■

Countless writings underlie the urgency for our modern world, with all its bustle and noise, of rediscovering the value of meditation, of silence, of prayer, of devotion. I preached it before I practiced it. If one is to help the world towards its rediscovery, one must practice it oneself. The religious life must be fed. We devote years to studying a trade or profession. Ought we show less perseverance in acquiring the experience of God?

Experiments have shown how much of our behavior is determined by the mental images to which our minds are constantly returning. If we bring our minds back again and again to God, we shall by the same inevitable law be gradually giving the central place to God, not only in our inner selves, but also in our practical everyday lives.

PAUL TOURNIER
Reflections from the Adventure of Living, 1965

OVERVIEW:

THE SIXTIES

1960–1969   Hope and Turmoil

The contrast between the social cohesion of the fifties and the social turbulence of the sixties could not have been more pronounced. The "noise of conflict" first heard in the twenties literally erupted in the sixties. Protests became the common denominator among vastly differing segments of society. From the civil rights protests in the early sixties to student antiwar protests later in the decade, this was a time of chaos, unrest, social consciousness, and sweeping legislation. Historians Lois and Alan Gordon describe the events of the sixties as a time when "social and political idealism challenged the materialistic values and conformity of the fifties with an energy that effected changes throughout the American scene."

This decade belonged to the young. Early rock 'n roll tunes of lovelorn angst evolved into the equivalent of a national soundtrack of a generation intent on change. Bob Dylan, Jimi Hendrix, Janis Joplin, the Beatles, and the Rolling Stones were only a few of those whose music gave expression to voices of dissent.

"The summer of 1965 is one of the most traumatic

moments in American history..." Martin Marty says. We sent troops to Viet Nam and saw Watts burn. We passed civil rights legislation and new immigration laws. The pluralism of future decades began with these events.

The 1960 election of John F. Kennedy, the first Roman Catholic to hold the country's highest office, marked the end of Protestant dominance as a defining cultural norm. In the wake of Vatican II, "dialogue" became the credo of the dominant religious traditions in the United States. America was moving toward diversity. Later decades would come to view the sixties as the beginning of what some theologians and historians call the post-Christian era in American religion.

■ ■ ■

The Decade at a Glance

- 1960   John F. Kennedy is elected.
- 1961   The Berlin wall is built.
- 1961   Freedom Rides are organized to promote racial integration on buses, trains, and in terminals.
- 1961   USSR puts first man in space, Yuri Gagarin. U.S. follows a month and a half later with Alan Shepard.
- 1961   Roger Maris of the New York Yankees breaks Babe Ruth's record by hitting 61 home runs in one season.
- 1962   John Glenn is the first American to orbit earth.

- 1962   Cuban missile crisis escalates the cold war.
- 1963   Publication of Betty Friedan's *The Feminine Mystique* marks the beginning of the feminist movement.
- 1963   Zip codes are instituted.
- 1964   The Olympics are telecast via satellite from Tokyo.
- 1964   Surgeon General issues the first cigarette warning.
- 1963   President John F. Kennedy is assassinated in Dallas. Lyndon B. Johnson is sworn in.
- 1964   Johnson signs the Civil Rights Act.
- 1964   Martin Luther King Jr. wins the Nobel Peace Prize.
- 1964   Johnson is re-elected.
- 1965   LBJ's peace offer is rejected; the Vietnam War escalates.
- 1965   More than 14,000 National Guardsmen control rioting in Watts, South Los Angeles.
- 1966   "Black Power" enters the civil rights movement, introducing the militancy of Stokely Carmichael.
- 1967   Detroit riot becomes largest U.S. riot of the century.
- 1967   *Apollo 1* blows up, killing three. Space program halts for several months.
- 1968   Richard Nixon is elected.
- 1968   Assassinations of Martin Luther King Jr. and Robert Kennedy.
- 1968   Computer RAM (random access memory) arrives on the market.
- 1969   Neil Armstrong walks on the moon.

■ ■ ■

Enduring Moments

And so, my fellow Americans: ask not what your country can do for you—ask what you can do for your country.

JOHN F. KENNEDY
Inaugural address, January 20, 1961

It may be true that the law cannot make a man love me, but it can keep him from lynching me, and I think that's pretty important.

MARTIN LUTHER KING JR.
The Wall Street Journal, November 13, 1962

I don't know what you can say about a day when you see four beautiful sunsets.... This is a little unusual, I think.

JOHN GLENN
Columbia Chronicles, 1962

Until justice is blind to color, until education is unaware of race, until opportunity is unconcerned with the color of men's skin, emancipation will be a proclamation but not a fact.

LYNDON B. JOHNSON
Address at Gettysburg, May 30, 1963

America wept tonight not alone for its dead young President, but for itself.... Somehow the worst prevailed over the best.

JAMES RESTON
Columbia Chronicles, 1963

The new electronic interdependence recreates the world in the image of a global village.

MARSHALL HERBERT MCLUHAN
The Medium Is the Message, 1967

Advertising treats all products with the reverence and the seriousness due to sacraments.

THOMAS MERTON
Conjectures of a Guilty Bystander, 1968

That's one small step for man, one giant leap for mankind.

NEIL ARMSTRONG
Televised broadcast, July 20, 1969

■　■　■

THE SIXTIES

(1960–1969)

VOICES OF THE DECADE:
Hope and Turmoil

To love at all is to be vulnerable. Love anything, and your heart will certainly be wrung and possibly be broken. If you want to make sure of keeping it intact, you must give your heart to no one.... Wrap it up carefully round with hobbies and little luxuries; avoid all entanglements; lock it up safe in the casket or coffin of your selfishness. But in that casket—safe, dark, motionless, airless—it will change. It will not be broken; it will become unbreakable, impenetrable, irredeemable.... The only place outside of Heaven where you can be perfectly safe from all the dangers and perturbations of love is Hell.

C. S. LEWIS
The Four Loves, 1960

■ ■ ■

Questions of faith are not like riddles or crossword puzzles: with things of this sort it may take one some time to find the solution, but once it's found, everything is clear and simple. It is completely different with the faith. Here we have, not human truth which men can state and understand, but God's truth, which goes far beyond any statement or understanding of man's. The faith never becomes clear. The faith remains obscure. Not until we enter into glory will it be otherwise: "We see now through a glass in a dark manner: but then face to face. Now I know in part: but then I shall know even as I am known" (1 Cor. 13: 12). Only when we are in glory will it be otherwise. Until then there will always be more difficulties coming up, more doubts coming up: there are bound to be. Doubt is the shadow cast by faith. One does not always notice it, but it is always there, though concealed. At any moment it may come into action. There is no mystery of the faith which is immune to doubt.

HANS KÜNG
That the World May Believe, 1963

■　■　■

I gain strength, courage, and confidence by every experience in which I must stop and look fear in the face.... I say to myself, I've lived through this and can take the next thing that comes along.... We must do the things we think we cannot do.

ELEANOR ROOSEVELT
You Learn by Living, 1960

■　■　■

When I seek to point people to Christ, it is because I am convinced that he alone is God's answer to life's deepest problems.

BILLY GRAHAM
"God's Hand on My Life," *Newsweek,* March 29, 1999

■ ■ ■

We sometimes have to listen, much to our regret, to voices of persons who, though burning with zeal...say that our era, in comparison with past eras, is getting worse.... We feel we must disagree with those prophets of gloom, who are always forecasting disaster, as though the end of the world was at hand.... Divine Providence is leading us to a new order of human relations which by men's own efforts, even beyond their very expectations, are directed towards the fulfillment of God's superior and inscrutable design. Everything, even human differences, leads to the greater good of the Church.

POPE JOHN XXIII
Address, Second Vatican Council, October 11, 1962

■ ■ ■

God guides us, despite our uncertainties and our vagueness, even through our failings and mistakes. He often starts us off to the left, only to bring us up in the end to the right; or else he brings us back to the right, after a long detour, because we started off by mistake to the left in the belief that we were obeying him. He leads us step by step, from event to event. Only afterwards, as we look back over the way we have come and reconsider certain important moments in our lives in the light of all that has followed them, or when we survey the whole progress of our lives, do we experience the feeling of having been led without knowing it, the feeling that God has mysteriously guided us.

PAUL TOURNIER
Reflections, 1965

■ ■ ■

Anyone who imagines he can simply begin meditating without praying for the desire and the grace to do so, will soon give up.

THOMAS MERTON
Spiritual Direction and Meditation, 1960

■ ■ ■

Give me a pure heart—that I may see Thee,
A humble heart—that I may hear Thee,
A heart of love—that I may serve Thee,
A heart of faith—that I may abide in Thee.

Thou takest the pen—and the lines dance.
Thou takest the flute—and the notes shimmer.

Thou takest the brush—and the colors sing.
So all things have meaning and beauty in that space
beyond time where Thou art.
How, then, can I hold back anything from Thee.

DAG HAMMARSKJÖLD
1964 diary entries, *Markings*, 1964

■ ■ ■

Try, with God's help, to perceive the connection—even physical
and natural—which binds your labour with the building of the
Kingdom of Heaven; try to realize that heaven itself smiles upon
you and, through your works, draws you to itself; then, as you
leave church for the noisy streets, you will remain with only one
feeling, that of continuing to immerse yourself in God.

Divine Milieu: An Essay on the Interior Life, 1960

We are not human beings having a spiritual experience. We are
spiritual beings having a human experience.

PIERRE TEILHARD DE CHARDIN
"Words for Quiet Moments," *Catholic Digest*

■ ■ ■

You should do your dead-level best to put goodness in your faith; wisdom in your goodness, self-control in your wisdom; patience in your self-control, godliness in your patience; brotherliness in your godliness, and love in your brotherliness.

No one has ever once caught a glimpse of God. Yet if we love everybody, God is present among us and his love is brought to maturity in us.

CLARENCE JORDAN
The Cotton Patch Version of Hebrews and the General Epistles, 1973

■ ■ ■

It was the year of Halley's Comet. I was a little boy living in a sawmill town in Florida. I had not seen the comet in the sky because my mother made me go to bed with the setting of the sun. Some of my friends who were more privileged had tried to convey to me their impression of the awe-inspiring spectacle. And I heard my stepfather say one day when he came home for lunch that a man had been down at the mill office selling what he called "comet pills." The theory was that if these pills were taken according to directions, when the tail of the comet struck the earth, the individual would be immune. As I remember it, the owner of the sawmill made several purchases, not only for himself and family, but for his key workmen—the idea being that after the debacle he would be able to start business over again.

One night I was awakened by my mother, who asked if I would like to see the comet. I got up, dressed quickly, and went out with her into the back yard. There I saw in the heavens the awesome tail of the comet and stood transfixed. With deep anxiety I asked, without taking my eyes off it, "What will happen to us when that thing falls out of the sky?" There was a long silence during which I felt the gentle pressure of her fingers on my shoulders; then I looked into her face and saw what I had seen on another occasion, when without knocking I had rushed into her room and found her in prayer. At last she said, "Nothing will happen to us, Howard. God will take care of us." In that moment something was touched and kindled in me, a quiet reassurance that has never quite deserted me. As I look back on it, what I sensed then was the fact that what stirred in me was one with what created and controlled the comet. It was this inarticulate awareness that silenced my fear and stilled my panic.

HOWARD THURMAN
Disciplines of the Spirit, 1963

■ ■ ■

Sometimes at that moment [in despair] a wave of light breaks into our darkness, and it is as though a voice were saying: "You are accepted. You are accepted, accepted by that which is greater than you."

PAUL TILLICH
The Shaking of the Foundations, 1948

■ ■ ■

When [Karl] Barth gave his Princeton lectures in 1962...it was announced that he would receive questions from the audience if the questions were written out beforehand. One of my students said he wouldn't dare ask Karl Barth a question! It would be, he hinted, like tangling with Socrates. "Why not?" I said. "Ask him whether he thinks it makes any difference where you begin to study theology." To my alarm, after one of the lectures, Barth read the student's question aloud and replied in words to the effect that, no, it doesn't make any difference where you start so long as Jesus Christ is at the center. It was also at this time, by the way, when someone asked Barth to distill the essence of his magnum opus in a few words,...he replied, "Jesus loves me—this I know, for the Bible tells me so."

KARL BARTH
As told by Hugh Kerr, *The Simple Gospel,* 1991

■ ■ ■

The last word which I have to say as a theologian and also as a politician is not a term like "grace," but a name, "Jesus Christ." *He* is grace, and he *is* the last, beyond the world and the church and even theology.... What I have been concerned to do in my long life has been increasingly to emphasize this name and to say: There is no salvation in any other name than this. For grace, too, is there. There, too, is the impulse to work, to struggle, and also the impulse towards fellowship, towards human solidarity. Everything that I have tested in my life, in weakness and in foolishness, is there. But it is there.

KARL BARTH
As told by Eberhard Busch, *Karl Barth,* 1968

■　■　■

FROM THE SPEECHES OF
MARTIN LUTHER KING JR.

I just want to do God's will. And He's allowed me to go up to the mountain. And I've looked over. And I've seen the promised land. I may not get there with you. But I want you to know tonight that we as a people will get to the promised land. And I'm happy tonight. I'm not worried about anything. I'm not fearing any man. Mine eyes have seen the glory of the coming of the Lord.

"I See the Promised Land," Memphis, April 3, 1968

I have a dream that one day this nation will rise up and live out the true meaning of its creed: "We hold these truths to be self-evident: that all men are created equal."

I have a dream that one day on the red hills of Georgia the sons of former slaves and the sons of former slaveowners will be able to sit down together at a table of brotherhood....

I have a dream that my four children will one day live in a nation where they will not be judged by the color of their skin but by the content of their character.

I have a dream today....

I have a dream that one day every valley shall be exalted, every hill and mountain shall be made low, the rough places will be made plain, and the crooked places will be made straight and the glory of the Lord shall be revealed, and all flesh shall see it together.

MARTIN LUTHER KING JR.
"I Have a Dream," August 28, 1963

OVERVIEW:

THE SEVENTIES

1970–1979   A Time of Transition

The ten years between the turbulent sixties and the materialistic eighties were years of transition, assimilation, and adaptation. This was, without a doubt, a decade of momentous events and unprecedented firsts: the first and only fatal use of military firepower against student protesters (at Kent State University in Ohio), first peacetime gas shortages, first American loss in a war, first resignation of a president. Nonetheless, the seventies lacked the enduring, unmistakable images and easy characterizations of other decades. In many ways this was a decade eclipsed by those before and after.

A new wave of immigration changed the face of America and brought a much greater diversity in religious traditions. Racial prejudice remained deeply ingrained, but legislation continued to pave the way for societal change. Segregation was finally illegal everywhere, and for the first time since the writing of the Constitution, the right to vote was guaranteed to all citizens. Barbara Jordan, a black woman, gave the keynote address at a presidential convention. Barbara Walters became the first woman to anchor a national nightly newscast. Diversity began to be valued rather than denigrated.

But as American society was integrating sweeping changes, conservative resistance was alive and well—both political and religious. Evangelical Christian books and music became multi-million dollar industries. Evangelist Billy Graham continued his widely attended crusades, and his popularity catapulted his books to the bestseller lists. The growing feminism of the decade was offset by the appeal of opposing voices from political crusader Phyllis Schlafly to *The Total Woman* sensation Marabel Morgan.

As the decade ended with double-digit inflation and soaring interest rates, the country was ready to move on.

■ ■ ■

The Decade at a Glance

- •1970   The floppy disc is introduced.
- •1970   *Apollo 13* lands safely after problems in orbit.
- •1970   Voting age is lowered to 18.
- •1970   First gay rights march occurs in New York City.
- •1971   2,000 Vietnam veterans protest by throwing their medals on the steps of Congress.
- •1972   Eleven Israeli athletes are killed by Arab terrorists at the Munich Olympics.
- •1972   HBO starts pay-for-cable service.
- •1972   Equal Rights Amendment passes Congress.

- 1972   Nixon is re-elected.
- 1973   Alaska Pipeline construction begins.
- 1973   *Roe v Wade* strikes down existing state anti-abortion laws.
- 1974   Hank Aaron breaks Babe Ruth's career home run record by hitting 715.
- 1974   Nixon resigns after Congress passes articles of impeachment following the Watergate investigation. Gerald Ford becomes president.
- 1975   Ford officially ends America's role in Vietnam.
- 1976   Jimmy Carter is elected president.
- 1976   Bicentennial of the U.S. is celebrated throughout the country.
- 1976   The Episcopal Church in the U.S. votes to ordain women.
- 1977   *Roots,* a television mini-series, is watched by 36 million Americans.
- 1977   *Star Wars* is released and breaks box-office records.
- 1978   A Polish Cardinal becomes Pope John Paul II, the first non-Italian pontiff in more than 450 years.
- 1978   The first test-tube baby is born in Great Britain.
- 1978   Jim Jones's Peoples Temple in Jonestown, Guyana, is the site of a mass suicide with 911 casualties.
- 1979   Students overtake the U.S. embassy in Iran, taking 100 American hostages.
- 1979   Israel-Egypt peace treaty is signed, ending a 30-year state of war.

■   ■   ■

Enduring Moments

Houston, we've had a problem.

JAMES LOVELL
Apollo 13 communication, 1970

I've suffered more as a woman than as a black.

SHIRLEY CHISHOLM
1971

Who has set us here, in this vocation, at this late date, out of due time? To ask the question is to imply an answer: there is a...Who, who has set; we have not accidentally fallen, we have been placed. As of course we already know in our marrow.

JOHN UPDIKE
A Month of Sundays, 1974

I think Vietnam was what we had instead of happy childhoods.

MICHAEL HERR
1977

We must adjust to changing times and still hold to unchanging principles.

JIMMY CARTER
Inaugural address, January 20, 1977
(Quoting his high school teacher Julia Coleman)

I don't know the key to success, but the key to failure is trying to please everybody.

BILL COSBY
Ebony, June, 1977

Life is difficult.
This is a great truth, one of the greatest truths.

M. SCOTT PECK
The Road Less Traveled 1978

There is something uniquely valuable that women and men bring to ordained ministry, and it has been distorted and defective as long as women have been debarred. Somehow men have been less human for this loss.

DESMOND TUTU
Crying in the Wilderness, 1978

■ ■ ■

THE SEVENTIES

(1970–1979)

VOICES OF THE DECADE:
A Time of Transition

Let us not be satisfied with just giving money. Money is not enough, money can be got, but they need your hearts to love them. So, spread love everywhere you go: first of all in your own home. Give love to your children, to your wife or husband, to a next-door neighbor.

MOTHER TERESA OF CALCUTTA
A Gift for God, 1974

■ ■ ■

No, brothers and sisters, it is not enough to change laws. You have to change hearts. Otherwise, when you have completed the journey of your social labors you shall find yourselves right back at the beginning—only this time it is you who will be the arrogant, the rich, and the exploiters of the poor.

This is why I took the Gospel path. For me the Gospel was the sign of liberation, yes, but of true liberation, the liberation of hearts. This was the thrust that lifted me out of the middle-class spirit, which is present in every age, and is known as self-ishness, arrogance, pride, sensuality, idolatry, and slavery.

CARLO CARRETTO
I, Francis, ca 1970

■ ■ ■

I would like to travel light on this journey of life, to get rid of the encumbrances I acquire each day....

The most difficult thing to let go is my *self,* that self which, coddled and cozened, becomes smaller as it becomes heavier. I don't understand how and why I come to be only as I lose myself, but I know from long experience that this is so.

MADELEINE L'ENGLE
The Irrational Season, 1977

■ ■ ■

The needed change within us is God's work, not ours. The demand is for an inside job, and only God can work from the inside. We cannot attain or earn this righteousness of the king-dom of God; it is a grace that is given....

In this regard it would be proper to speak of "the path of dis-ciplined grace." It is "grace" because it is free; it is "disciplined" because there is something for us to do.... The grace of God is unearned and unearnable, but if we ever expect to grow in grace, we must pay the price of a consciously chosen course of action.

■ ■ ■

Prayer catapults us onto the frontier of the spiritual life. Of all the Spiritual Disciplines prayer is the most central....Meditation introduces us to the spiritual life...study transforms our minds, but it is the Discipline of prayer that brings us into the deepest and highest work of the human spirit. Real prayer is life creating and life changing....

■ ■ ■

To pray is to change.

RICHARD FOSTER
Celebration of Discipline: The Path to Spiritual Growth, 1978

■ ■ ■

Faith is better understood as a verb than as a noun, as a process than as a possession. It is an on-again-off-again rather than once-and-for-all. Faith is not being sure where you're going but going anyway. A journey without maps. Tillich said that doubt isn't the opposite of faith; it is an element of faith.

Grace is something you can never get but only be given. There's no way to earn it or deserve it or bring it about any more than you can deserve the taste of raspberries and cream or earn good looks or bring about your own birth.

A good night sleep is grace and so are good dreams. Most tears are grace. The smell of rain is grace. Somebody loving you is grace. Have you ever *tried* to love somebody?

A crucial eccentricity of the Christian faith is the assertion that people are saved by grace. There's nothing *you* have to do. There's nothing you *have* to do. There's nothing you have to *do*.

The grace of God means something like: Here is your life. You might never have been, but you *are* because the party wouldn't have been complete without you. Here is the world. Beautiful and terrible things will happen. Don't be afraid. I am with you. Nothing can ever separate us. It's for you I created the universe. I love you.

There's only one catch. Like any other gift, the gift of grace can be yours only if you'll reach out and take it.

Maybe being able to reach out and take it is a gift too.

FREDERICK BUECHNER
Wishful Thinking, 1973

■ ■ ■

Our idea of God tells us more about ourselves than about Him.

We must learn to realize that the love of God seeks us in every situation, and seeks our good.

To live in communion, in genuine dialogue with others is absolutely necessary if man is to remain human.

THOMAS MERTON
New Seeds of Contemplation, 1961

■ ■ ■

How easy it is for me to live with you, Lord!
How easy it is for me to believe in you!
When my mind is distraught and my reason fails,
When the cleverest people do not see further than this
  evening what must be done tomorrow
You grant me the clear confidence
  that you exist, and that you will take care
  that not all the ways of goodness are stopped.
  At the height of earthly fame I gaze with wonder at
  that path through hopelessness—
  to this point from which even I have been able
  to convey to men some reflection of the Light
  which comes from you.

And you will enable me to go on doing
as much as needs to be done.

ALEXANDER SOLZHENITSYN
Solzhenitsyn: A Pictoral Record, 1974

■ ■ ■

FROM THE WRITINGS OF BILLY GRAHAM

Every circumstance, every turn of destiny, is for your good. It is working together for completeness. His plan for you is being perfected. All things working together for your good and for His glory.

Day-By-Day with Billy Graham, 1976

All the masterpieces of art contain both light and shadow. A happy life is not one filled only with sunshine, but one which uses both light and shadow to produce beauty.

BILLY GRAHAM
Day-By-Day with Billy Graham, 1976

■ ■ ■

Sometimes...you need to give people something that's for them, not just something that makes you feel good giving it.

KATHERINE PATERSON
Bridge to Terabithia, 1977

■ ■ ■

When we think about the people who have given us hope and have increased the strength of our soul, we might discover that they were not the advice givers, warners, or moralists, but the few who were able to articulate in words and actions the human condition in which we participate.... Not because of any solution they offered but because of the courage to enter so deeply into human suffering and speak from there. Neither Kierkegaard nor Satre nor Camus nor Hammarskjöld nor Solzhenitsyn has offered solutions, but many who read their words find new strength to pursue their own personal search. Those who do not run away from our pains but touch them with compassion bring healing and new strength.... In our solution-oriented [world] it is more important than ever to realize that wanting to alleviate pain without sharing it is like wanting to save a child from a burning house without the risk of being hurt.

HENRI J. M. NOUWEN
Reaching Out, 1975

■ ■ ■

I have tried and I cannot find, either in Scripture or history, a strong-willed individual whom God used greatly until He allowed them to be hurt deeply.

■ ■ ■

COURAGE.... It's just another word for inner strength, presence of mind against odds, determination to hang in there, to venture, persevere, and withstand hardship. It's got keeping power.... It's what makes the amputee reject pity and continue to take life by the throat. It's what forces every married couple having trouble *never* to say, "Let's terminate." It's what encourages the divorcee to face tomorrow. It's what upholds the young mother with kids in spite of a personal energy crisis.... Every day, in some way, your courage will be tested. Your test may be as simple as saying, "No," as uneventful as facing a pile of dirty laundry, or as unknown and unheralded as an inner struggle between right and wrong. God's medal-of-honor winners are made in secret because most of their courageous acts occur deep down inside.

A little girl lost a playmate in death and one day reported to her family that she had gone to comfort the sorrowing mother. "What did you say?" asked her father. "Nothing," she replied. "I just climbed up on her lap and cried with her."

CHARLES R. SWINDOLL
Killing Giants, Pulling Thorns, 1978

■ ■ ■

We must never forget that today's legendary achievements—
awesome as they may seem—were yesterday's risky adventures.
Courage is not the capacity never to be afraid; as Karl Barth
reminds us, "Courage is fear that has said its prayers."

Despair is always presumptous. How do we know what lies in
the Great Not Yet or how some present "evil" may work itself
out as a blessing in disguise?

Be patient before I label any experience or close the door of
hope. Despair is presumption, pure and simple, a going beyond
what the facts at hand should warrant.... The worst thing is
never the last thing. God is already working on Plan B even as
Plan A lies in shambles around our feet.

JOHN R. CLAYPOOL
adapted from *Tracks of a Fellow Struggler,* 1974

■ ■ ■

The media in general, and TV in particular, are incomparably
the greatest single influence in our society today. This influence
is, in my opinion, largely exerted irresponsibly, arbitrarily, and
without reference to any moral or intellectual, still less spiritual
guidelines whatsoever.

MALCOLM MUGGERIDGE
Christ in the Media, 1977

■ ■ ■

All my life I labored for success, wealth, acceptance, and power. The more I obtained, the less I discovered I had. Surrendering everything in absolute brokenness, however, was the beginning of finding the identity and purpose for which I had battled so hard. In giving up my life to Christ, I had found it....

If God depended on our perfection, He would be the captive of His creation and not God at all.

CHARLES COLSON
Life Sentence, 1979

OVERVIEW:

THE EIGHTIES

1980–1989
Culture Wars and Material Dreams

The eighties brought quite a dramatic turn in public mood, political agendas, and cultural mores. Reaganomics—not since the days of FDR had a president's name been so closely linked to the economic policies of a decade. Reading *The Wall Street Journal,* heading off to aerobics classes, crunching spreadsheets on personal computers, and eating "lite" foods led the national trends. *Glasnost* and *perestroika* were new words that carried with them the power to break up the Soviet Union.

The "yuppie" decade of the eighties ushered in a time of rampant materialism, from designer purses to designer underwear. Americans developed preferences for expensive food items and forty percent of every food dollar was spent eating out. The video game craze began in earnest when Pac Man machines showed up in 1980. We had become, unequivocally, a high-tech, multimedia society, with cable TV, electronic games, personal computers, and the Internet.

Ronald Reagan's landslide victory in the 1980 presidential election came with the entry of the religious right into the political arena in the most public, aggressive manner since the Scopes trial in the 1920s. Conservative Christianity returned with fervor to the political arena as Jerry Falwell's Moral Majority and James Dobson's Focus on the Family asserted powerful political influence, but no single voice defined American religion.

The changing role of women in American religion emerged as a major development. Women were now writing, teaching, and producing much of the spiritual literature. "The ordination of women in the Protestant mainline denominations and women working outside the home as well as in the home may be the single biggest revolution in history as far as long-range religious implications are concerned," Marty says.

■ ■ ■

The Decade at a Glance

- •1980   United States boycotts the Olympics in Moscow.
- •1980   CNN launches the first 24-hour news channel.
- •1980   AIDS virus is identified.
- •1981   Iranian hostages are released after 444 days.
- •1981   Sandra Day O'Connor becomes first woman Supreme Court Justice.
- •1981   In England, Prince Charles weds Lady Diana.

- **1982** Personal computer prices plummet as high-tech industries begin lay-offs for the first time.
- **1983** The mandated break-up of AT&T gives rise to various "Baby Bells."
- **1984** Reagan is re-elected.
- **1985** "Crack," a cocaine derivative, becomes available, increasing drug abuse and related street violence.
- **1986** The space shuttle *Challenger* explodes 73 seconds after lift-off. All aboard are killed, including the first civilian passenger, Christa McAuliffe.
- **1986** A nuclear accident at the Chernobyl nuclear plant in the Ukraine spews radioactive waste over much of Europe.
- **1986** U.S. officially observes Martin Luther King Jr. Day for the first time.
- **1988** George Bush is elected.
- **1989** Friday, October 13, the Dow drops 190.58 points, second worst drop in history.
- **1989** Decade ends with the reunification of East and West Germany after the Berlin Wall, a symbol of Communist oppression, comes down.

■　■　■

Enduring Moments

Life was a lot simpler when what we honored was father and mother rather than all major credit cards.

ROBERT ORBEN
The Wall Street Journal, March 17, 1980

———————

Are you better off than you were four years ago?

RONALD REAGAN
Televised debate with Jimmy Carter, 1980

———————

We just want to remind people that there are guys without arms and legs lying in that hospital right now who never got a parade.... Where are the yellow ribbons for them?

GREGORY STEELE
Vietnam veteran, 1981
(referring to the yellow ribbons used to show support for the Iranian hostages)

———————

None of us really understands what is going on with all these numbers.

DAVID STOCKMAN
U.S. Office of Management and Budget, 1981

———————

People don't start wars, governments do.

RONALD REAGAN
Time, March 18, 1985

Although he's regularly asked to do so, God does not take sides in American politics.

GEORGE J. MITCHELL
Iran-Contra hearings, July 13, 1987

We are a nation of communities...all of them varied, voluntary, and unique...a brilliant diversity spread like stars, like a thousand points of light in a broad and peaceful sky.

GEORGE BUSH
Acceptance address, Republican National Convention, 1988

When I look out at this convention, I see the face of America, red, yellow, brown, black, and white. We are all precious in God's sight—the real rainbow coalition.

JESSE JACKSON
Address, Democratic National Convention, 1988

■ ■ ■

THE EIGHTIES

(1980–1989)

That day, a day of the following summer, Miss White and I knelt in her yard while she showed me a magnifying glass. It was a large, strong hand lens. She lifted my hand and, holding it very still, focused a dab of sunshine on my palm. The glowing crescent wobbled, spread, and finally contracted to a point. It burned; I was burned; I ripped my hand away and ran home crying. Miss White called after me, sorry, explaining, but I didn't look back.

Even now I wonder: if I meet God, will he take and hold my bare hand in his, and focus his eye on my palm, and kindle that spot and let me burn?

But no. It is I who misunderstood everything and let everybody down. Miss White, God, I am sorry I ran from you. I am still running, running from that knowledge, that eye, that love from which there is no refuge. For you meant only love, and love, and I felt only fear, and pain. So once in Israel love came to us incarnate, stood in the doorway between two worlds, and we were all afraid.

ANNIE DILLARD
Teaching a Stone to Talk, 1982

A real answer to the question, "My God, why have you forsaken me?" cannot be a theoretical answer beginning with the word "Because." It has to be a practical answer....

Our disappointments, our lonelinesses, and our defeats do not separate us from him; they draw us more deeply into communion with him. And with the final unanswered cry, "Why, my God, why?" we join in his death cry and await with him the resurrection.

This is what faith really is: believing, not with the head or the lips or out of habit, but believing *with one's whole life*. It means seeking community with the human Christ in every situation in life, and in every situation experiencing his own history.

JÜRGEN MOLTMANN
The Power of the Powerless, 1983

■　■　■

Before the world was made, when it was only darkness and mist and waters, God was well aware of Lake Wobegon, my family, our house, and He had me all sketched out down to what size my feet would be (big), which bike I would ride (a Schwinn), and the five ears of corn I'd eat for supper that night. He had meant me to be there; it was His Will, which it was up to me to discover the rest of and obey, but the first part—being me, in

Lake Wobegon—He had brought about as He had hung the stars and decided on blue for the sky.

GARRISON KEILLOR
Lake Wobegon, 1985

■ ■ ■

Some people evaluate history as moving...toward a broader humanity, a deeper justice, a more caring relation with the environment, a greater intimacy between persons. That depends, I suppose, on how you read it. I do not hope in these things in the sense that I "hope in God." If anything is going to be redemptive, it will have to be in virtue of God in strange ways working out his purposes with his creation which, it is my faith, he does not abandon. So my hope is in God....

I do not believe that our relationship to the earth is liable to change for the better until it gets catastrophically worse. Our record indicates that we can walk with our eyes wide open straight into sheer destruction if there is a profit on the way— and that seems to me to be what we are doing now. I have no great expectation that human cussedness will somehow be quickly modified and turned into generosity or that humanity's care of the earth will improve much.

But I do go around planting trees on the campus.

■ ■ ■

In marriage people may have differences and periods of weariness and boredom, but they have also built up an axis of relationships that constitutes a steady center....

There's a story by Flannery O'Connor in which she tells about an old couple who had lived in the Appalachians all their lives in a little cabin overlooking the opposite mountain. They were sitting there—both very aged people—in their rocking chairs on a spring day. The man said, "Well, Sarah, I see there's still some snow up there on the mountain." Now he knew there was snow on the mountain every year. She knew there was snow every year. So why does he have to say it? Because to perceive that, to know at times there is snow and at times there is not snow—this was part of the observation of an eternal rhythm which made their life together. In marriage you say the same things over and over, you inquire about the same people; and this is ho-hum in one way. But it is breathtaking in another.

JOSEPH A. SITTLER
Grace Notes and Other Fragments, 1981

■ ■ ■

When you fail to be what you want so much to be to one another, I pray that you will realize that pain, tragedy, and sin are not interruptions to a good Christian marriage. They are part of the absolute fabric of every good Christian marriage.

So you don't have to run away from them. I pray that you'll embrace them, ask forgiveness, and give forgiveness, as hard as that will be...knowing that through the power of faith in Jesus Christ, God changes these forgiven sins and hurts into wisdom, understanding, and the ability to love which Jesus Christ came to give us.

J. KEITH MILLER
Unpublished sermon, September 20, 1980

■ ■ ■

Taking your children to school and kissing your wife goodbye. Eating lunch with a friend. Trying to do a decent day's work. Hearing the rain patter against the window. There is no event so commonplace but that God is present within it, always hiddenly, always leaving you room to recognize him or not to recognize him, but all the more fascinatingly because of that, all the more compellingly and hauntingly.... If I were called upon to state in a few words the essence of everything I was trying to say both as a novelist and as a preacher, it would be something like this: Listen to your life. See it for the fathomless mystery that it is. In the boredom and pain of it no less than in the excitement and gladness: touch, taste, smell your way to the holy and hidden heart of it because in the last analysis all moments are key moments and life itself is grace.

FREDERICK BUECHNER
Now and Then, 1983

■ ■ ■

Creativity is not the work of a few. We each carry within us the image of God the Creator; we each have the task of making the earth into a fairer, kinder place. The first step is imagining a better world, and that is most apt to happen when we suffer or look on suffering.

ELIZABETH O'CONNOR
Cry Pain, Cry Hope, 1987

■ ■ ■

Jesus does not respond to our worry-filled way of living by saying that we should not be so busy with worldly affairs. He does not try to pull us away from the many events, activities, and people that make up our lives....

He asks us to shift the point of gravity, to relocate the center of our attention, to change our priorities.... Jesus does not speak about a change of activities, a change in contacts, or even a change of pace. He speaks about a change of heart.

HENRI J. M. NOUWEN
Making All Things New, 1981

We must be willing to get rid of the life we've planned, so as to have the life that is waiting for us.

JOSEPH CAMPBELL
The Joseph Campbell Companion, 1991

■ ■ ■

I had rather attempt something great and fail, than to attempt nothing at all and succeed.

ROBERT SCHULLER
"The Truth About Failure," *Tough Times Never Last, But Tough People Do!,* 1984

■ ■ ■

If you are preoccupied with people who are talking about the poor, you scarcely have time to talk to the poor. Some people talk about hunger, but *they* don't come and say, "Mother, here is five rupees. Buy food for these people." But they can give a most beautiful lecture on hunger.

I had the most extraordinary experience once in Bombay. There was a big conference about hunger. I was supposed to go to that meeting and I lost the way. Suddenly I came to that place, and right in front of the door to where hundreds of people were talking about food and hunger, I found a dying man. I took him out and I took him home.

He died there.

He died of hunger.

And the people inside were talking about how in 15 years we will have so much food, so much this, so much that, and that man died.

See the difference?

MOTHER TERESA OF CALCUTTA
Words to Love By, 1983

■ ■ ■

There is a moment between intending to pray and actually praying that is as dark and silent as any moment in our lives. It is the split second between thinking about praying and really praying. For some of us, this split second may last for decades. It seems, then, that the greatest obstacle to prayer is the simple matter of beginning, the simple exertion of will, the starting, the acting, the doing. How easy it is, and yet—between us and the possibility of prayer there seems to be a great gulf fixed: an abyss of our own making that separates us from God.

EMILIE GRIFFIN
Clinging: The Experience of Prayer, 1984

■ ■ ■

Listen to me, Lord,
as a Mother,
and hold me warm,
and forgive me.
Soften my experiences
into wisdom,
my pride
into acceptance,
my longing
into trust,
and soften me
into love....

TED LODER
Guerrillas of Grace, 1984

■ ■ ■

It is not insignificant that my first apprehension of the love of God was granted in an experience with my father. Nor is it generally uncommon that God is apprehended in experience. Nor, in fact, can the divine and human meeting happen any other way. God is not a God of the pulpit, though the pulpit proclaim him. He is a God in and of the histories of humankind.

What is significant is that I should have to say so.

WALTER WANGERIN JR.
Ragman and Other Cries of Faith, 1984

I think the Christian view of the world is especially well suited to laughter. For the Christian, life is ultimately a comedy, not a tragedy. I am using comedy in its highest and oldest sense, as a story with a happy ending. Christians believe in a happy ending. Despite the presence of great suffering and evil in the world, we believe that God is bending the arc of human history toward redemption. He is in the process of redeeming his creation. Evil and death were defeated at Calvary and—miracle of miracles—all shall be well. This is a view of life that promotes healthy laughter.

Laughter is, I think, literally a gift of God. It may even be part of what it means to be made in God's image. We can laugh because God does.

Healthy laughter is a shared experience of a moment of joy.... It can also reflect a needed recognition of our own short-comings, foolishness, and failure....

It is a common mistake to think that comedy and laughter are not serious. This is not true at all.... Not only is comedy at the heart of the Christian vision of reality, but laughter and suffering are often closely linked....

There is, of course, a perverted version of all good things. Healthy laughter accepts, celebrates, heals, and unifies.

DANIEL TAYLOR
Letters to My Children, 1989

OVERVIEW:

THE NINETIES

1990–1999   The Decade of Diversity

The last decade of the twentieth century was punctuated by headlines describing a world that would have been incomprehensible during the first decade. Words like *globalization, virtual reality, political correctness, new age, smart bombs, school shooting sprees, Y2K,* and *www.com* became part of the cultural fabric of America during the nineties.

From megachurches to on-line chat rooms, America's definition of community changed. Consider just a few statistics compiled by historians Lois and Alan Gordon: An estimated 15 million, including smokers, cross-dressers, alcoholics, sexual compulsives, and gamblers attended weekly self-help groups; fewer Americans married in 1990 than in any year since 1965; 73 percent of mothers with children between the ages of 6 and 17 were employed.

As a nation, our awareness of our cultural, political, and religious diversity increased. Even anglo-saxon, "old stock" Americans developed an increasing appreciation for their immigrant roots. Author Anna Quindlen wrote in *The New York*

Times, "It is foolish to forget where you came from, and that, in the case of the United States, is almost always somewhere else."

A nation in which the greatest percentage of the population claims belief in God had undergone a radical shift in how that belief in God was expressed, understood, and experienced. Long-standing religious traditions were eroded by eclectic, individualistic, "cafeteria-style" spirituality. *USA Today* reported that, "Never have Americans been more at ease talking about spirituality—or less loyal to the institutions that perpetuate it."

With the approach of the millennium came the challenge of finding some equilibrium between our social cohesion as a nation and the diversity that emerged from individuality.

■ ■ ■

The Decade at a Glance

- •1990 Four white Los Angeles police officers are indicted for beating black motorist Rodney King.
- •1991 "Operation Desert Storm" leads to Allied forces' attacking Iraq. All regular television programming is canceled for live coverage of the Gulf War.
- •1991 The economy officially goes into recession for the first time since 1982.
- •1991 The VCR becomes the fastest selling appliance in U.S. history.
- •1991 *Beauty and the Beast* becomes the first animated film to win the Oscar for best picture.

- **1992** William Clinton is elected president.
- **1993** Thirty-three percent of Americans work from home.
- **1993** PLO leader Yasser Arafat and Israeli Prime Minister Yitzhak Rabin sign a peace agreement.
- **1994** The Anglican Church ordains women priests.
- **1994** Former football star O. J. Simpson is charged and later acquitted of criminal charges in the murder of his ex-wife and her friend.
- **1995** The Alfred P. Murrah Federal Building in Oklahoma is bombed.
- **1996** Clinton is re-elected.
- **1996** Congress passes sweeping legislation revamping the nation's welfare system.
- **1997** The world mourns the deaths of Princess Diana and Mother Teresa, both international humanitarians.
- **1997** China takes control of Hong Kong after 150 years of British control.
- **1997** Scottish geneticists successfully clone an adult sheep.
- **1998** For only the third time in our nation's history, Congress impeaches the President but fails to convict him.
- **1998** Mark McGwire of the St. Louis Cardinals breaks Roger Maris's record by hitting 70 home runs in one season.
- **1999** In Texas, for the first time in the history of the South, a white man is given the death penalty for the lynching-style killing of a black man.

Enduring Moments

Somewhere out in this audience may even be someone who will one day follow in my footsteps, and preside over the White House as the president's spouse. I wish him well!

BARBARA BUSH
Wellesley College commencement address, 1990

I'm bothered by so many people who are so sure what God is up to, who God is, even what God looks like. There was never that kind of certainty in the beginning.

WILL CAMPBELL
Questions of Faith: Contemporary Thinkers Respond, 1990

Know the difference between success and fame. Success is Mother Teresa. Fame is Madonna.

ERMA BOMBECK
1991

When there was a disaster, it used to be that people went to church and all held hands.... Now the minute anything happens they run to CNN.

DON HEWITT
ca. 1991

Can we get along?

RODNEY KING
After the riot that followed his nationally televised beating, 1992

Be bold and courageous. When you look back on your life, you'll regret the things you didn't do more than the ones you did.

H. JACKSON BROWN JR.
Life's Little Instruction Book, 1992

Why did you offer us sneakers if you could give us scholarships?

FIFTH-GRADER ANDRES RODRIGUEZ
after Donald Trump offered to buy Nike sneakers for the students at his school, 1997

Women are actually in charge of everything. The game of chess in the perfect example: where the king is kind of the figurehead but the queen is the most powerful piece on the board. Life is not unlike that.

WILL SMITH
USA Weekend, November 20–22, 1998

■ ■ ■

THE NINETIES

(1990–1999)

VOICES OF THE DECADE:
The Decade of Diversity

I note the obvious differences
between each sort and type,
But we are more alike, my friends,
than we are unalike.

MAYA ANGELOU
"The Human Family," *I Shall Not Be Moved,* 1990

■ ■ ■

A keen sense of humor helps us to overlook the unbecoming, understand the unconventional, tolerate the unpleasant, overcome the unexpected, and outlast the unbearable.

BILLY GRAHAM
The Reader's Digest, March 1993

■ ■ ■

Children thrive best in an atmosphere of genuine love, undergirded by reasonable, consistent discipline.... Loving discipline works! It stimulates tender affection, made possible by *mutual* respect between a parent and a child. It bridges the gap which otherwise separates family members who should love and trust each other.

JAMES DOBSON
The New Dare to Discipline, 1992

■ ■ ■

If there is not laughter in intimacy, it becomes heavy, burdensome, and dull. At my best moments, the love dialogue I try to carry on with You each day is comic—what could be more comic than a human addressing the Ground of Being as an intimate? It's a kind of blasphemy that I dare because You have called for it, and that is pretty humorous too.

ANDREW M. GREELEY
Love Affair: A Prayer Journal, 1992

■ ■ ■

Care of the soul is quite different in scope from most modern notions of psychology and psychotherapy. It isn't about curing, fixing, changing, adjusting, or making healthy, and it isn't about some idea of perfection or even improvement. It doesn't look to the future for an ideal, trouble-free existence. Rather, it remains patiently in the present, close to life as it presents itself day by day, and yet at the same time mindful of religion and spirituality.

THOMAS MOORE
Care of the Soul, 1992

[The poor] have a role to play in building a society truly worthy of the human person—a society in which none are so poor that they have nothing to give and none are so rich that they have nothing to receive.

POPE JOHN PAUL II
Speech, 1995

■ ■ ■

There was, indeed, something I had missed about Christianity, and now all of a sudden I could see what it was. It was the Resurrection! How could I have been a church historian and a person of prayer who loved God and still not known that the most fundamental Christian reality is not the suffering of the cross but the life it brings?... The foundation of the universe for which God made us, to which God draws us, and in which God keeps us is not death, but joy.

ROBERTA BONDI
Memories of God, 1995

■ ■ ■

God answers our prayers. Sometimes the answer is yes. Sometimes the answer is no. Sometimes the answer is, you've got to be kidding!

JIMMY CARTER
Interview, CNN, November 18, 1997

■ ■ ■

Jesus could weep. Sometimes when you look at the ugliness that makes you weep, you know that the heart of God is also weeping. Jesus is for real. He does not give up on anyone, least of all on me.

DESMOND TUTU
Questions of Faith: Contemporary Thinkers Respond, 1990

■ ■ ■

Our task on earth is singular—to choose our eternal home. You can afford many wrong choices in life. You can choose the wrong career and survive, the wrong city and survive, the wrong house and survive. You can even choose the wrong mate and survive. But there is one choice that must be made correctly, and that is your eternal destiny.

MAX LUCADO
And the Angels Were Silent, 1992

■ ■ ■

Where were you, God of kindness, in Auschwitz? What was going on in heaven, at the celestial tribunal, while your children were marked for humiliation, isolation, and death only because they were Jewish?

These questions have been haunting me for more than five decades....

At one point, I began wondering whether I was not unfair with you. After all, Auschwitz was not something that came down ready-made from heaven. It was conceived by men, implemented by men, staffed by men. And their aim was to destoy not only us but you as well. Ought we not to think of your pain, too? Watching your children suffer at the hands of your other children, haven't you also suffered?

Let us make up, Master of the Universe.

In spite of everything that happened? Yes in spite. Let us make up: For the child in me, it is unbearable to be divorced from you so long.

ELIE WIESEL
The New York Times, October 2, 1997

■ ■ ■

Everything that God has created is potentially holy, and our task as humans is to find that holiness in seemingly unholy situations. When we can do this, we will have learned to nurture our souls.

Think about it: It's easy to see God's beauty in a glorious sunset or in ocean waves crashing on a beach. But can we find the holiness in a struggle for life?...

We must remember that everything in this world has God's fingerprints on it—that alone makes it special. Our inability to see beauty doesn't suggest in the slightest that it is not there. Rather, it suggests that we are not looking carefully enough or with broad enough perspective to see it.

When our life is filled with the desire to see the holiness in everyday things, something magical begins to happen: ordinary life becomes extraordinary, and the very process of living begins to nourish our soul! As long as we can find even a kernel of holiness in a situation, our soul will grow and feel cared for....

The idea is to find some bit of holiness in everything—food, sex, earning and spending money, having children, conversations with friends. Everything can be seen as a miracle, as part of God's plan. When we can truly see this, we nourish our souls.

HAROLD KUSHNER
Handbook for the Soul, 1995

■ ■ ■

Cautious lest we let our hopes soar, only later to see some dashed; bruised because we have been hurt; and realistic because of past setbacks, we quite naturally may be guarded in our emotions.

Then a voice from within us may say, "Be careful about being exuberant, about laughing. If you dance, shuffle; don't leap. If you make music, be muted. Be careful about your pace; you might stumble. Keep your fingers crossed. Being joyful is risky business."

Then a voice from without us will say, "Let go. Let your spirit be released. Sing confidently. Grow flowers and smell and pick and give some. Spin the wheel blithely as you shape a vase. Create delicate traceries and be joyful, joyful."

Not only do we cheat ourselves and those around us if we are only glum or always wary when it comes time to respond to divine stirrings. No, we are then also being simply unfaithful to the surrounding reality. The one who purges gloom has given occasions and reasons, in the midst of life's sadness, to be joyful.

MARTIN MARTY
Our Hope for Years to Come, 1995

■ ■ ■

I have found that among its other benefits, giving liberates the soul of the giver....

When we cast our bread upon the waters, we can presume that someone downstream whose face we will never know will benefit from our action, as we who are downstream from another will profit from that grantor's gift.

Our bounty, once decided upon, should be without concern, overflowing one minute and forgotten the next....

When we give cheerfully and accept gratefully, everyone is blessed.

MAYA ANGELOU
Wouldn't Take Nothing for My Journey Now, 1996

■ ■ ■

Working with children on the writing of poetry has led me to ponder the ways that most of us become exiled from the certainties of childhood; how it is that the things we most treasure when we're young are exactly those things we come to spurn as teenagers and young adults. Very small children are often conscious of God, for example, in ways that adults seldom are. They sing to God, they talk to God, they recognize divine presence in the world around them.... Yet these budding theologians often despise church by the time they're in eighth grade.

In a similar way, the children who un-selfconsciously make up songs and poems when they're young—I once observed a three-year-old singing a passionate ode to the colorful vegetables in a supermarket—quickly come to regard poetry as meaningless and irrelevant.... I wonder if children don't begin to reject both poetry and religion for similar reasons, because the way both are taught takes the life out of them. If we teach children when they're young to reject their epiphanies, then it's no wonder that we end up with so many adults who are...poetically and theologically illiterate.

KATHLEEN NORRIS
The Cloister Walk, 1996

■ ■ ■

I am a cheerful man, even in the dark, and it's all thanks to a good Lutheran mother.... Mother was well composed, a true

Lutheran, and taught me to Cheer up, Make yourself useful, Mind your manners, and above all, Don't feel sorry for yourself.

GARRISON KEILLOR
Wobegon Boy, 1997

■ ■ ■

God will not force Himself upon us against our will. If we want His love, we need to believe in Him. We need to make a definite, positive act of commitment and surrender to the love of God. No one can do it for us.

BILLY GRAHAM
Breakfast with Billy Graham, 1996

■ ■ ■

All I ask you to do today is open "the eyes of your eyes" and give your life another glance. Are your basic needs met? Do you have a home? Food on the table? Clothes to wear? Is there a regular paycheck coming in? Do you have dreams? Do you have your health? Can you walk, talk, see the beauty that surrounds you, listen to music that stirs your soul or makes your feet want to boogie? Do you have family and friends whom you love and who love you?

Then pause a moment and give thanks. Let your heart awaken to the transforming power of gratefulness.

SARAH BAN BREATHNACH
Simple Abundance, 1995

I think that, regardless of our culture, age, or even personal handicaps, we can still strive for something exceptional. Why not expand our sights instead of restricting our lives and accepting the lowest common denominator of a dormant existence? Faith...will permit us to take a chance on a new path, perhaps different from the one we now follow. It may be surprising where it leads.

JIMMY CARTER
The Virtues of Aging, 1998

■ ■ ■

Most of the people I know who have what I want—which is to say, purpose, heart, balance, gratitude, joy—are people with a deep sense of spirituality.... They follow a brighter light than the glimmer of their own candle; they are part of something beautiful. I saw something once...that said, "A human life is like a single letter of the alphabet. It can be meaningless. Or it can be a part of a great meaning."

ANNE LAMOTT
Traveling Mercies: Some Thoughts on Faith, 1999

■ ■ ■

All I want to say this morning I can sum up in a story told to me by a colleague years ago. When Nelson was five years old he started to kindergarten. About October the teacher of the class asked the children, "Would you like to make something with your hands as a Christmas gift for your parents?" My friend was at the time a pipe smoker, so his little son said, "I'd like to make my father an ashtray." The teacher got him some clay and helped his little hands work the clay into the rough shape of an ashtray....

At every succeeding step in this process, the little son's excitement increased....

The last day before the Christmas holidays came, and the school had the usual Christmas pageant with all the parents in attendance. When it was over, the little boy went to his schoolroom to get his carefully wrapped package. But in the excitement of putting on his coat and running down the hall, waving goodbye to his friends, he inadvertently tripped. The precious package went up in the air and came crashing down on the floor with a terrible sound of breaking. The work of the autumn and the hopes of Christmas Day were absolutely dashed. The boy began to weep as if it were the end of everything.

My friend has a military background. It made him very uncomfortable, he told me, to see a male child of his crying in public. So what does he do? He walks over the the little fellow who is dissolved in tears and says like some Prussian general, "Don't cry son. Doesn't matter, doesn't really make any difference."

"Of course it matters!" his wife exclaimed, pushing him aside. She was much closer to the ways of the heart than he. "Of course it matters when something this precious has been broken." And with that she caught up the weeping child in her arms and began to weep with him, in the weeping that is always appropriate when we break things that are precious.

My friend said that he watched in wonder as that feminine image of God did two incredible things. She reached into her purse and got her handkerchief and began to wipe the tears from the little boy's eyes and from her own face. Then she said with real strength, "Come on, son. Let's pick up the pieces and take them home, and see what we can make of what is left."

In that little family drama, we see the options that are open to us when we have tragically and inexcusably failed. We can try to deny the significance of what we have done, as my friend did. But denial empties everything of meaning. If our failures don't mean anything, then nothing means anything. Or, we can cry as if our mistakes are absolutely hopeless. "Three strikes and you're out" is the current mode of saying that once you have made a mistake you are disqualified forever. Or we can take the approach of that holy mother, who entered into the crucible of her son's sufferings, as we need to do, but then dared to say,

"Come on. Let's pick up the pieces, take them home and see what we can make of what is left."

That is the gift of *next time*.... It is God's voice to every one of [us]....

JOHN R. CLAYPOOL
"Next Time," 1995

BIBLIOGRAPHY

While every effort has been made to secure permission we may have failed in a few cases to trace or contact the copyright holder. We apologize for any inadvertent oversight or error.

Angelou, Maya, "The Human Family," *I Shall Not Be Moved,* © 1990 by Maya Angelou. Reprinted by permission of Random House, Inc.; *Wouldn't Take Nothing for My Journey Now,* © 1993 by Maya Angelou. Reprinted by permission of Random House, Inc.

Auden, W. H., "For the Time Being: A Christmas Oratorio" in *Collected Poems,* ed. Edward Mendelson (New York: Random House, © 1976 by the executors of the Estate of W. H. Auden), p. 308.

Baillie, John, *A Diary of Private Prayer* (New York: Charles Scribner's Sons, 1949, copyright renewed 1977 by Ian Fowler Baillie).

Ban Breathnach, Sarah, *Simple Abundance,* (New York: Warner Books, 1995), January 13, © 1995 by Sarah Ban Breathnach. Quote from January 13 by permission of Warner Books Inc.

Barth, Karl, *Church Dogmatics, vol. II, part 1* (Edinburgh: T. & T. Clark, 1957) p. 655; *Church Dogmatics, vol. III, part 2* (Edinburgh: T. & T. Clark, 1960), p. 539.

Bondi, Roberta C., *Memories of God* (Nashville: Abingdon, © 1995), p. 170.

Bonhoeffer, Dietrich, *Letters and Papers From Prison* (Reprinted with the permission of Simon & Schuster, Inc.© 1953, 1967, 1971 by SCM Press, Ltd.), pp. 289, 311-312; *Cost of Discipleship* (New York: Macmillan Publishing Co., first paperback edition 1963), trans. 1937, first ed. 1949.

Buechner, Frederick, *Wishful Thinking: A Theological A & C,* © 1973 by Frederick Buechner. Reprinted by permission of HarperCollins Publishers, Inc., pp. 25, 33, 34; *Now and Then* © 1973 by Frederick Buechner. Reprinted by permission of HarperCollins Publishers, Inc., 1983), p. 87.

Busch, Eberhard, *Karl Barth: His Life from Letters and Autobiographical Texts,* English translation by John Bowden, © SCM Press and Fortress Press 1976. Reissued 1994 by Wm. B. Eerdmans.

Buttrick, George A., *The Interpreter's Dictionary of the Bible* (New York: Abingdon Press, 1962).

Byrd, Richard E., *Alone* (G. P. Putnam's Sons, © 1938 by Richard E. Byrd).

Campbell, Joseph, A *Joseph Campbell Companion* (New York: HarperCollins, 1991).

Carlo Carretto, *I, Francis* (English trans. copyright © 1982 by Orbis Books, Maryknoll, NY 10545). Used by permission of Orbis Books.

Carter, Jimmy, Larry King television interview, CNN, November 18, 1997, quoted in *Quotationary,* Leonard Roy Frank, ed., (New York: Random House, 1999), p. 635; *The Virtues of Aging,* large print ed., (New York: Random House in association with Ballantine Publishing Group, div. Random House, 1998), pp. 92, 126.

Chambers, Oswald, *My Utmost for His Highest* (New York: Dodd, Mead & Company, Inc., 1935).

Chesterton, G. K., *William Blake,* 1910; *Heretics,* 1905; *Robert Browning,* 1903; *What's Wrong With the World,* 1910; "Conversations," summer 1910; *Appreciations and Criticisms of the Works of Charles Dickens,* (New York: E. P. Dutton, 1911).

Claypool, John, *Tracks of a Fellow Struggler,* (Waco, TX: Word Books, 1974), p. 33.

Colson, Charles, *Life Sentence* (Lincoln, VA: Chosen Books, 1979) p. 291.

Day, Dorothy, "Love and ever more love" originally from *House of Hospitality,* Dorothy Day: Selected Writings, edited by Robert Ellsberg, © 1983, 1992 by Robert Ellsberg and Tamar Hennessey. Published in 1992 by Orbis Books, Maryknoll, NY 11545.

Dillard, Annie, *Teaching a Stone to Talk,* © 1982 by Annie Dillard. Reprinted by permission of HarperCollins Publishers, Inc., p. 139.

Dobson, James C., *The New Dare to Discipline* (Tyndale House, © 1970, 1992 by James C. Dobson).

Du Bois, W. E. B., *Black Reconstruction in America, 1860-1880,* reprinted with the permission of Scribner, a Division of Simon & Schuster Inc., © 1935, 1962 W. E. Burghardt Du Bois, p. 18.

Einstein, Albert, *Out of My Later Years* (New York: Philosophical Library, 1950).

Eliot, T. S., *Selected Essays* (Harcourt Brace, 1927); *A Dialogue on Dramatic Poetry* (Harcourt Brace, 1928); "Little Gidding," *Four Quartets* (Harcourt Brace, 1943).

Fosdick, Harry Emerson, *A Guide To Understanding the Bible* (New York: Harper, 1938), p. 69; Radio address, January 6, 1946 as quoted in *Light from Many Lamps* (New York: Simon and Schuster, 1951, renewed 1979), pp. 49-50.

Foster, Richard J., *Celebration of Discipline: The Path to Spiritual Growth,* by Richard J. Foster. Reprinted by permission of HarperCollins Publishers, Inc., pp. 6-8, 33.

Fox, Emmet, *Your Heart's Desire* (California: De Vorss & Co., © 1961, 1922); *The Seven Day Mental Diet* (New York: Church of the Healing Christ, 1935); *The Lord's Prayer* (publisher unknown), p. 182.

Frankl, Viktor E., *Man's Search for Meaning,* ©1959, 1962, 1981, 1992 by Viktor E. Frankl. Reprinted by permission of Beacon Press, Boston.

Frost, Robert, "Fire and Ice," *The Poetry of Robert Frost* (New York: Holt, Rinehart and Winston, 1969, © 1923), p. 220.

Graham, Billy, *World Aflame* (Garden City, NY: Doubleday & Company, Inc., 1965), p. 83; *Day-By-Day with Billy Graham* (Minneapolis: World Wide Press, 1976), February 11 and June 5; *Breakfast with Billy Graham* (Ann Arbor, MI: Servant Publications © 1996), frontispiece.

Griffin, Emilie, *Clinging: The Experience of Prayer* (New York: Harper & Row, 1984), p. 1.

Hammarskjöld, Dag, *Markings,* trans., Auden/Sjoberg, © 1964 by Alfred A. Knopf Inc. and Faber & Faber Ltd. Reprinted by permission of Alfred A. Knopf Inc., pp. 35, 56, 84, 89, 118, 120.

Holmes Jr., Oliver Wendell, *Speeches* (Little, Brown & Company).

John XXIII (Pope), *Modern Christian Thought: From the Enlightenment to Vatican II,* James C. Livingston, ed., (New York: Macmillan Publishing Co., Inc., 1971), p. 492.

Johnson, James Weldon, "Listen, Lord—A Prayer," *God's Trombones* (New York: Viking Press, 1927, renewed 1955 by Grace Nail Johnson, Viking Compass Edition, 1969), p. 13.

Keillor, Garrison, *Lake Wobegon Days,* © 1985 by Garrison Keillor. Used by permission of Viking Penguin, a division of Penguin Putnam, Inc., p. 12; *Wobegon Boy* (New York: Viking, 1997), p. 1.

Keller, Helen, *Midstream,* © 1929 by Helen Keller and the Crowell Publishing Company. Used by permission of Doubleday, a division of Random House, Inc.; *The Unconquered* (documentary), 1955.

Kelly, Thomas R., *A Testament of Devotion,* © 1941 by Harper & Row Publishers, Inc. Renewed 1969 by Lois Lael Kelly Stabler. New introduction © 1992 by HarperCollins Publishers, Inc. Reprinted by permission of HarperCollins Publishers, Inc.

King, Martin Luther, Jr., *A Testament of Hope,* "I Have a Dream" (1963) and "I See the Promised Land" (1968). Reprinted by arrangement with The Heirs to the Estate of Martin Luther King, Jr., c/o Writers House. © 1968 by Martin Luther King, Jr., © renewed 1996 by The Estate of Martin Luther King, Jr.

Küng, Hans, *That the World May Believe,* 1963. Reprinted by permission of Sheed & Ward, an apostolate of the Priests of the Sacred Heart. 7373 S. Lovers Lane Road, Franklin, Wisc. 53132. 1-800-558-0580.

Kushner, Rabbi Harold, *Handbook for the Soul,* © 1995 by Harold S. Kushner, edited by Richard Carlson. Originally published by Little Brown & Co. Reprinted by permission of Curtis Brown Ltd.

L'Engle, Madeleine, *The Irrational Season,* ©1977 by Crosswills Ltd. Reprinted by permission of HarperCollins Publishers, Inc., pp. 116–119.

Lewis, C. S., *Mere Christianity* (New York: Macmillan Publishing Company, 1943); "Charity" in *The Four Loves,* © 1960 by Helen Joy Lewis and renewed 1988 by Arthur Owen Bayfield, Adapted by permission of Harcourt, Inc., p. 169.

Loder, Ted, *Guerrillas of Grace: Prayers for the Battle* (San Diego: LuraMedia, 1984), pp. 16, 81, 92.

Lindbergh, Anne Morrow, *Gift from the Sea,* © 1955, 1975, renewed 1983 by Anne Morrow Lindbergh. Reprinted by permission of Pantheon Books, a division of Random House, Inc., pp. 23, 29.

Lucado, Max, *And the Angels Were Silent* (Portland, OR: Multnomah, 1992).

Marshall, Catherine, *A Man Called Peter* (New York: McGraw-Hill, 1951).

Marshall, Peter, *The Prayers of Peter Marshall,* edited by Catherine Marshall, © 1949, 1982. Published by Chosen Books, a division of Baker Book House, Grand Rapids, MI., pp. 228, 243.

Marty, Martin, *Our Hope for Years to Come* (Minneapolis: Augsburg Fortress, 1995), p. 88.

McKim, Randolph, *Modern American Religion, Vol. 1: The Irony of It All,* by Martin Marty, (Chicago: The University of Chicago, 1986), p. 301.

Merton, Thomas, *New Seeds of Contemplation,* Reprinted by permission of New Direction Publishing Corp. © 1961 by the Abbey of Gethsemani, Inc., pp. 15, 55; *Spiritual Direction and Meditation* (Collegeville, MN: Liturgical Press, 1960), p. 68; *Thoughts in Solitude,* 1958 by Abbey of Gethsemani. Copyright renewed © 1986 by the trustees of the Thomas Merton Legacy Trust. Reprinted by permission of Farrar, Straus and Giroux, LLC.

Moltmann, Jürgen, *The Power of the Powerless,* English translation © 1983 by SCM Press Ltd. Reprinted by permission of HarperCollins Publishers, Inc., pp. 119-120.

Moore, Thomas, *Care of the Soul,* © 1992 by Thomas Moore. Reprinted by permission of HarperCollins Publishers, Inc., 1992, p. xv.

Niebuhr, Reinhold, *Leaves from the Notebook of a Tamed Cynic* (Louisville, KY: Westminster/John Knox Press). Used by permission; *Reflections on the End of an Era* (New York: C. Scribner's Sons, 1934).

Norris, Kathleen, *The Cloister Walk* (New York: Riverhead Books, a division of G. P. Putnam's Sons, 1996), p. 60.

Nouwen, Henri J. M., *Reaching Out,* © 1975 by Henri J. M. Nouwen. Used by permission of Doubleday, a division of Random House, Inc.,

p. 43; *Making All Things New: An Invitation to the Spiritual Life,* ©
1981 by Henri Nouwen. Reprinted by permission of HarperCollins
Publishers, Inc., pp. 41–42.

O'Connor, Elizabeth, *Cry Pain, Cry Hope* (Waco: Word, 1987), Used by
permission of Potter's House Book Service, p. 57.

O'Connor, Flannery, "The Fiction Writer and His Country," *The Living
Novel: A Symposium* (New York: Macmillan, 1957).

Paterson, Katherine, *Bridge to Terabithia* (New York: Harper/Trophy,
1977), p. 125.

Peale, Norman Vincent, *Treasury of Joy and Enthusiasm,* © 1981 by Norman
Vincent Peale. Published by Fleming H. Revell, a division of Baker
Book House Co., Grand Rapids, Mi.

Pickford, Mary, *Why Not Try God?,* © 1934, Mary Pickford, H. C. Kinsey
& Co., Inc.

Rauschenbusch, Walter, *The Social Principles of Jesus,* 1916, (1977 reprint
New York: Norwood).

Sayers, Dorothy, *Unpopular Opinions* (New York: Harcourt, Brace & Co.,
1947), p. 148.

Schuller, Robert, "The Truth About Failure," *Tough Times Never Last, but
Tough People Do!* (Thomas Nelson, © 1983).

Schweitzer, Albert, *The Quest of the Historical Jesus* (London: A. and C.
Black, 1922); *The Private Letters between Albert Schweitzer and Helene
Bresslau,* trans. Antje B. Lemke, February 26, 1905.

Seuss, Dr. (Theodor Seuss Geisel), *Horton Hears a Who,* ™ and © 1954 and
renewed 1982 by Dr. Seuss Enterprises, L.P. Reprinted by permission
of Random House, Inc.

Sheen, Fulton, *Peace of Soul* (New York: McGraw-Hill, 1949).

Sitler, Joseph A., *Grace Notes and Other Fragments,* © 1981 Fortress Press. Used by permission of Augsburg Fortress.

Solzhenitsyn, Alexander, *Solzhenitsyn: A Pictorial Record* (New York: Farrar, Straus & Giroux, 1974).

Sunday, Billy (Ellis, William T.) *Billy Sunday: The Man and His Message* (Philadelphia: The John C. Winston Co., 1917), pp. 40, 57, 77.

Swindoll, Charles R., *Killing Giants, Pulling Thorns,* (Grand Rapids, MI: Zondervan Publishing Co., 1978).

Taylor, Daniel, *Letters to My Children,* © 1989 by Daniel Taylor. Used by permission of InterVarsity Press, P.O. Box 1400, Downers Grove, IL 60515, pp. 116-17.

Teilhard de Chardin, Pierre, *Divine Milieu: An Essay on the Interior Life* (Wm. Collins Sons & Co. and Harper & Row, 1960).

Teresa, Mother, A Gift for God (New York: Harper & Row, © 1975 by Mother Teresa, Missionaries of Charity); Words to Love By, © 1983 by Ave Maria Press, P.O. Box 428, Notre Dame, IN 46556. Used with permission of the publisher.

Thurman, Howard, *Disciplines of the Spirit,* © 1987 by Howard Thurman (Richmond, IN: Friends United Press edition, 1987), p. 86-87.

Tillich, Paul, *The Shaking of the Foundations* (New York: Scribner's Sons, 1948).

Tournier, Paul, *Reflections from the Adventure of Living,* © 1965 by Paul Tournier. Reprinted by permission of HarperCollins Publishers, Inc.

Tozer, A. W., *The Pursuit of God* (Camp Hill, PA: Christian Publications, 1982, 1993). Used by permission of the publisher.

Tutu, Desmond, *Questions of Faith: Contemporary Thinkers Respond,* by Dolly K. Patterson, ed. (Philadelphia, PA: Trinity Press International, 1990), p. 54.

Underhill, Evelyn, *The Spiritual Life,* © 1937 by Hodder & Stoughton. Used by permission. pp. 24.

W., Bill, (co-founder of AA) Alcoholics Anonymous (New York: Alcoholics Anonymous World Services, Inc., Third Edition, 33rd printing, © 1939). The material excerpted from pages 9-11, 13-14 of the book *Alcoholics Anonymous* is reprinted with permission of Alcoholics Anonymous World Services, Inc. Permission to reprint the material does not mean that AA has reviewed or approved the contents of this publication, nor that AA agrees with the views expressed herein. AA is a program of recovery from alcoholism only—use of AA material in connection with non-AA programs and activities, or use in any other non-AA context, does not imply otherwise.

Wangerin, Walter, Jr., *Ragman and Other Cries of Faith,* (HarperSanFrancisco, © 1984 by Walter Wangerin Jr.), p. 71.

Washington, Booker T., *Up From Slavery: An Autobiography,* (Garden City, NY: Doubleday, 1963), pp. 293, 300.

Wiesel, Elie, "Forgiving God's Silence at Auschwitz," © 1997 by *New York Times,* October 2, 1997, p. A19. Reprinted by permission.

Williams, Margery, *The Velveteen Rabbit,* (New York: Alfred A. Knopf, 1984) pp. 12–14.

Wolfe, W. Beran, *How to Be Happy Though Human,* © 1931 by W. Beran Wolfe and reprinted by permission of Rinehart & Co., Inc.

Index